THE

RESURRECTION OF THE DEAD:

A VINDICATION OF THE

LITERAL RESURRECTION OF THE HUMAN BODY;

IN OPPOSITION TO

THE WORK OF PROFESSOR BUSH.

By Calvin Kingsley.

Contend earnestly for the faith once delivered to the saints.—*Jude*

GEORGE PECK, EDITOR.

New-York:
PUBLISHED BY CARLTON & PHILLIPS,
200 MULBERRY-STREET.
1855.

ADVERTISEMENT.

The following pages contain the substance of a discourse on the resurrection of the body, preached in Erie, Pa., late in the fall of 1845. The occasion of the sermon was the introduction of numerous copies of a book written by George Bush, Professor of Hebrew in the New-York University. The avowed object of the book is to overthrow the commonly received opinion of the resurrection of the body. These books were extensively circulated and read. Some embraced the new theory, others found their faith weakened by the bewildering speculations of the learned author.

Under these circumstances, believing the error inculcated in the book to be fundamental; that it aimed a fatal blow at the very vitals of Christianity; that it led directly, in all its tendencies, to infidelity; a *refutation* was undertaken, and the following discourse, in three parts, delivered during three successive sabbaths.

Immediately upon the delivery of the sermon, the author was waited on for a copy of his discourse for publication. But owing to providential circumstances the sermon could not be prepared for the press at that time, nor during the past winter.

A few weeks since, the author learned from his much esteemed friend, Hon. James D. Dunlap, of Erie, that while at Harrisburgh, the last winter, he had made arrangements with the book agents at New-York to publish the sermon, provided that, in the estimation of the agents, it answered the description given of it; and forthwith he commenced writing out the discourse, from extensive notes prepared at the time of preaching it.

If the author were persuaded that his humble effort to defend the Scripture doctrine on the subject of the resurrection would have the effect, in any degree, to counteract the injurious tendencies of a theory, calculated at once to unsettle the very foundations of our holy Christianity; if it should have the effect in any degree to place in a clear light a great and precious doctrine of the gospel, and to rescue a truth that is *vital* from the attack of a vain philosophy, the same motive that led to its preparation and delivery would now induce him to give it a more extensive circulation.

Alleghany College, May 27, 1846.

THE

RESURRECTION OF THE DEAD.

PART I.

WHY SHOULD IT BE THOUGHT A THING INCREDIBLE WITH YOU, THAT GOD SHOULD RAISE THE DEAD?—ACTS XXVI, 8.

WHATEVER throws light upon the ultimate destination of man must be matter of intense interest to every considerate mind. That man is mortal; that his stay upon earth is brief and uncertain; that age, like the chilling winter, palsies and benumbs his limbs; that the dark and dismal night of death closes around him in the midst of his pursuits, are truths within the observation of all. But "if a man die, shall he live again?" Is there a trans-sepulchral world? Is the lamp of reason and intelligence, which has been lighted up by the eternal Fountain, to go out in everlasting darkness; or, does the curtain of death but conceal from mortal view its lustre, while it passes over the "gloomy vale" into a "spirit land?" Is the "dark valley and shadow of death" the ultimate boundary of human prospects, or is there beyond it "a land inhabited?" And, if so, what are the relations and dependencies between that world and this? These are questions which press upon the mind whose only illumination is the light of reason, with painful interest. These are problems belonging to a higher science than is taught in nature's book. A revelation from God alone can solve them. This has been made. The great Master and Teacher, "the Father of lights," has explained these otherwise inextricable mysteries, for our learning and salvation.

This revelation teaches most clearly,

I. That man's soul is immortal; that it does not die with the body, but has a conscious existence when the body is dead.

II. That although the body is *now* mortal, it was not originally so; but has become so by transgression.

III. That the body, which has become mor tal in consequence of sin, shall be raised again to life, and be made immortal, through the atonement of Jesus Christ; and,

IV. That soul and body united shall be happy or miserable for ever, in the world to come, according to the character sustained in this.

Every one of these propositions has been denied by those who, nevertheless, profess to believe the Scriptures. Yet not one of them can be disproved without doing violence to every known principle of interpretation.

But the third proposition, namely, that there will be a resurrection of the human body, will more particularly claim our attention at this time. Every fundamental doctrine of the Scriptures has, by turns, been assailed by the enemies or the misguided friends of the gospel of Christ; and the errors of these enemies or misguided friends have only been exposed by bringing the steady light of revelation to bear upon them, until their uncouth features and frightful deformities might be made apparent, and their evil and pernicious influence effectually shunned.

The time has come when in regard to the doctrine of the resurrection it is necessary to "contend earnestly for the faith once delivered to the saints." Professor Bush, a man of talent, of learning, and a minister of the gospel, has, in a very labored treatise, used all his strength and ingenuity to prove that there can be no resurrection of the human body, in any sense whatever. From the position Professor B. occupies, as well as from the relation his views have to certain other doctrines of Scripture, it is not difficult to foresee that his opinions will draw after him numerous followers.

A few quotations, from the work of Professor B., will show that I have not misunderstood him. On the first page of the preface he says: "The resurrection of the body, if my reasoning and expositions are well founded, *is not a doctrine of revelation.*" Again: "*The resurrection of the same body, in any sense whatever, encounters difficulties in our view absolutely insurmountable.*" P. 40. Again: "How the evidence adduced may strike the reader we know not; to our minds it is amply sufficient to establish the conclusion, that the resurrection of the body is not a doctrine sanctioned by reason or revelation, so far as we have hitherto interrogated the testimony of each." P. 274. Multitudes of such passages, from all parts of the book, might be collected.

Having seen what our author positively denies, let us next see what he positively affirms; that both denial and affirmation may be submitted to the test of the Scriptures. On page 70 he says, "The resurrection body is that part of our present being to which the essential life of the man pertains. We may not be able to see it, to handle it, to analyze, or describe it. But we know that it exists, because we know that we ourselves exist. It constitutes the inner, essential vitalities of our present bodies; and it lives again in another state, *because it never dies.* It is immortal in its own nature, and is called a body—a spiritual body—because the poverty of human language, or perhaps the weakness of the human mind, forbids the adoption of any more befitting term by which to express it." Again: "It would seem, then, on the whole, from a collation of all the grounds on which an opinion is founded, that the judgment of reason would be, that a spiritual body is *developed at death*—by the development we mean disengagement." P. 78. Again: "It is something essentially connected with vital operations; something that is exhaled with the dying breath, or, in other words, that goes from the body before it is consigned to the dust." Again: "Let it (the resurrection) be understood as an event which transpires with every individual believer, as soon as he leaves the body." P. 170. "The true anastasis (or resurrection) is the development of a spiritual body *at death.*" P. 78.

From these passages, which might be greatly extended, this theory maintains that all the resurrection there is for human beings, is the separation of the soul and body, at death; and the conscious existence of the soul, after death: the participation of the body in this resurrection being distinctly denied. That Professor B. means the same thing by his spiritual body which others mean by the soul is further evident from the following quotation, p. 145: "The prevailing sense of *resurrection*, in the New Testament, is simply that of a future existence, the future state, or immortality." Consequently by this theory there will be no general resurrection, nor general judgment: and this he argues at length in his book. "The grand point," says Professor B., "which we combat throughout, is that which affirms that no resurrection can take place but by means of the reunion of those principles, soul and body, which constitute our being in the present life. We maintain, on the other hand, that neither reason nor revelation countenance the idea of any such reunion. All the purposes of a future state of existence and retribution we contend may be answered without it." P. 78.

Having stated, somewhat at length, the theory which contradicts a great, and, as we believe, a fundamental doctrine of the Scriptures, let us next look at the arguments by which the new theory is substantiated. These are drawn, first, from reason; and, secondly, from revelation.

But the argument from reason is made the *criterion* by which the declarations of Scripture are interpreted. This will be made plain by another quotation, p. 385: "The point that will probably be regarded as most exceptionable, is the making our rational deductions the *criterion* in regard to the *meaning of the inspired* word, on a theme of so much importance as the mode of our future existence." Such a declaration, from such a quarter, cannot fail to startle the pious believer, who has been accustomed to place implicit reliance in the lively oracles of eternal truth. It is easy to perceive in this, though perhaps not so intended by the author, the latent germ of infidelity. And although it is but a smooth, round egg, a *serpent* is forming within it, whose poisonous venom will be the destruction of those who embrace him. The following quotation will show him more distinctly: "If the *letter* of revelation holds forth a view of the *doctrine* which arrays itself against the clearest evidence of *facts,* and the soundest process of reasoning, is there no demand, on the other side, for the reconciliation of Scripture with reason and science? *Are we to hoodwink our faculties to do homage to revelation?*" Here the more than semi-transparent covering shows us the snaky folds of the serpent. He is *full-*

blooded, if not *full-grown;* and ere long he will burst the shell, and become a hideous monster, rolling his fiery eyes, and darting his forked tongue. I would not charge the author of the new theory with intentionally advocating infidel principles, for he avows his firm belief in the Scriptures; but I *do* say that the legitimate tendency of such dealing with the Scriptures is to infidelity. What infidel would refuse to subscribe to the Scriptures, if permitted to reject, or explain away, whatever does not suit his "rational deductions?" and especially if he be allowed to do what Professor B. has done, positively contradict the inspired apostles, and accuse them of being *mistaken*, when they cross his path. It has been in precisely this way that many of the most ruinous and soul-destroying heresies have crept into the Christian church. Universalism and Unitarianism owe their very existence to this method of tampering with the Scriptures. Professor B. rejects the doctrine of the resurrection, because he cannot see any use for such a doctrine; affirming that all the purposes of a future state and of retribution may be answered without it. P. 78. For the same reason do Universalists deny the doctrine of future retribution. They suppose all the purposes of the divine government can be answered without it. For the same reasons do both Unitarians and Universalists deny the doctrine of a vicarious atonement, the divinity of Christ, and the doctrine of the Trinity. In all this there is such a show of philosophy, falsely so called, such a pampering of human pride, such erroneous notions of the true province of human reason, as are well calculated to induce those under the influence of such views to sit unblushingly in judgment on the ways of God. How has Professor B. ascertained that all the purposes of a future state can be answered without the resurrection of the human body? How likely are we to be mistaken, and to form erroneous opinions, in regard to things immediately surrounding us; and who, unless it be the crazy Swedenborg, with whose writings I suspect our author has kept company too long, shall stand up and declare that from his knowledge of all the relations and dependencies of a future state, as well as from his knowledge of all the purposes of the divine mind, there is no use for the human body in a future state?

I would not say that human reason has nothing to do in matters of religion; very far from it. Its sphere is, first, to examine the proofs which establish the authenticity of the Scriptures; and, secondly, to ascertain, by the established principles of interpretation, what the Bible *does teach*—not what it *must* teach, in order to accord with our previous notions or "rational deductions."

The very fact that a revelation has been made supposes human reason ignorant of the things revealed; otherwise there would have been no need of the revelation. That any particular doctrine of revelation cannot be discovered by the light of reason, therefore, is no objection against such doctrine, but rather an argument in its favor, inasmuch as if all the doctrines of the Bible might have been known without a revelation, there would have been more grounds for believing the Bible to be a mere human production, the result of man's "rational deductions."

The grand error in the theory we are opposing is, that it attempts to discover the doctrines of religion independently of the only light that has revealed them, and then requires the Bible to sanction its conclusions. The best eye cannot see without light. No more can the best reasoning powers draw correct conclusions without sufficient data. And in matters of re ligion it is the peculiar province of revelation to furnish this data. The optician who should shut himself up in a dark room, in order to investigate the properties of light, and then require the laws of optics to conform to his preconceived theory, his "rational" or irrational "deductions," would not be more inconsistent than the theologian who professes to investigate the deep things of God, independently of the only means that has revealed them, and then requires the Bible, whether it will or not, to sanction his favorite theology.

From all this it is a most "*rational* deduction," that human reason should investigate *any subject in the light of that science which properly embraces that subject.* What would be thought of the mathematician who should set himself to work to discover, by *arithmetical formula*, the laws of *chemical affinity?* or of the musician who should undertake to investigate the principles of *geometry* by *tones* and *semi-tones?* Can the laws of gravitation develop the principles of moral obligation? or the rules of rhetoric explain the properties of the rainbow? The reason is plain; these sciences are not homogeneous. They differ essentially in their nature, and the principles of the one do not apply to the other. Chemistry must be studied in the light of chemistry; geometry in the light of geometry, and so of all others.

Many truths can be demonstrated only by

the evidence of *experience*, and no previous train of reasoning *a priori* could develop them. A person takes into his mouth a little *starch*, a perfectly tasteless substance: he then tastes sulphuric acid, one of the most intensely sour and acrid of all substances. What does he expect will be the taste of the *compound* of the two? Why, inasmuch as the one was intensely sour, and the other had no taste at all, he would most likely conclude that the compound would be sour still. What then becomes of his "rational deductions" when, upon tasting the compound, he finds it *sugar*.

Take another example. A philosopher who has never seen a bird upon the wing, finds the nest of an eagle. He is told that from these eggs there will emerge animals which will move off with great rapidity through the air. The thing appears to him at once "incredible." He breaks one of the eggs, examines it minutely, ascertains its specific gravity to be even greater than water. Even if it should ever have life, of which he sees no signs, how is it going to move off in the air when it sinks in water? At length an animal, different from anything he has seen, emerges from the shell. He watches its growth and development until it is full grown. But yet its specific gravity is much greater than air.

How then is it going to rise and float off above the earth? While he thus reasons and speculates, the bird spreads his wings, and mounting above the clouds, mocks all his short-sighted speculations.

What a pity that men will not learn modesty from their own liability to be mistaken in matters much less mysterious than the resurrection of the dead! And if one human science cannot develop the principles of another human science, how much less shall any human science develop the great truths of revealed religion! It is true that the sciences reciprocally reflect light upon each other; and revelation sheds its effulgent light upon all true science; and all science, truly so called, reflects back the golden rays of revelation. But all this is incidental, and I may add, too, *providential;* but it is not the province of one science to develop another, much less is it the province of any or all human science to discover the great principles of divinely inspired truth.

As our author has drawn largely from the analogies of science in order to prepare the minds of his readers for his new theory, I now proceed to examine a sophism, which is at the very foundation of this new theory of the resurrection. It is argued that all knowledge is *progressive*, as well the knowledge of revelation; as the knowledge of the sciences and that, consequently, we may expect that different views will be entertained on the subject of revealed truth, in different ages, in accordance with this view of progressive knowledge. The various changes rung upon this idea occupy a large space in this modern theory. Now the *sophistry* does not consist in the mere assertion that "knowledge is progressive," but in the *application* of it. It is true that knowledge is progressive. But how does knowledge progress? By exploding at each successive step all previous knowledge? Most certainly not. It only progresses by ascertaining some *fixed principles*, and then proceeding upon these principles, and not by constantly *unsettling* these *principles themselves*. Truths must exist as unchangeable realities, before there can be any progressive knowledge of them. The knowledge of the sciences is progressive; but no progressive knowledge unsettles the great fundamental principles which are at the very foundation of the sciences themselves. For example, we may say the knowledge of geometry is progressive. But will any progressive knowlege of this science unsettle its elementary principles? Will any progressive knowledge prove that a square has not all its sides equal, and all its angles right-angles? or that a circle is not bounded by a curved line, every part of which is equally distant from a common point? And when it is fairly demonstrated that the square upon the hypothenuse of a right-angled triangle is equal to the sum of the squares of the other two sides, can any subsequent progressive knowledge prove this theorem false? Subsequent investigations thenceforth receive this theorem as an established truth. Similar reasoning applies to other sciences.

The case is similar with regard to revealed religion. God has established a system of truth, a religious science, for the salvation of mankind.

This science, like all others, contains certain elementary and fundamental truths, which truths remain unaltered by any progression in human knowledge. The resurrection of the dead is one of these truths, and one of so much importance, that our Saviour rests upon it his entire claim as Redeemer of the world. This doctrine comes to us as a revealed truth, and is, perhaps, more purely within the province of revelation alone, than almost any other doctrine of the Scriptures; a doctrine so entirely above and beyond the reach of unaided human reason, that she is unable in her own name to say one word either for or against it; but yet a doctrine as unequivocally taught in the Bible, the only book that could reveal it, as any proposition can be taught in language; and a doctrine of so much importance in the estimation of the inspired apostles, who understood by it, according to the admission of Professor B., the resurrection of the body, that they rested all their pretensions upon it, and even the salvation of their souls from eternal perdition; and suffered death in the most frightful forms, because they could not be made to renounce it. Nay more, Professor B., p. 167, admits that our Saviour intended that the apostles should believe this doctrine. If the God of truth intended that the apostles should believe this doctrine, how does Professor B. know but that he intends that all the rest of mankind should also believe it? If the unchangeable God intended that this doctrine should be believed eighteen centuries ago, how has Professor B. ascertained that he does not intend it still? Has there been any new revelation since? But Professor B. intends that mankind shall *disbelieve* this doctrine. May not his task, in this respect, be rather a thankless one? And is there not a little danger that he be found contending against God? If the doctrine was true when God intended it to be believed, it is true still. If it was false, then God intended that the apostles, who were made the dispensatories of his will to mankind, should believe a falsehood!! A conclusion at once both shocking and basphemous. How then is the law of progressive knowledge to strike from the bright constellation of religious truths this central star?

The truths of revelation are not like some *machines*, which require to be *remodeled* and *improved* from time to time in order to suit the improvements of the age; nor like some garments, that must be cut and made over every six months to be in fashion. If they were, there might be some propriety in talking about the law of progressive knowledge, as applied to the doctrine of the resurrection. Then, indeed, we might send to the east every spring and fall for our *theology*, as we now do for our *fashions.* But the doctrines of the gospel are pure, *unchanging*, and eternal truths.

There is no doubt that the knowledge of the Scriptures, like other knowledge, is progressive; and that age after age may unfold new excellences in the word of God, as its precepts come to be better obeyed, and its prophecies, yet future, come to be fulfilled and better understood; but so far from unsettling the confidence of mankind in its great fundamental truths, this very circumstance will but strengthen it.

We are now prepared to explode another sophism similar in its character to the one just examined. The principle laid down, out of which a great deal of capital is attempted to be made in all parts of the book, against the resurrection of the body, is, in substance, this: *The God of revelation is also* the God of *nature*, and the revelation in his *word* cannot contradict the revelation in his *works*. And our author cannot "*hoodwink* his *faculties* to do homage to revelation."

This popular declaration is in the mouth of every one who wishes to array his favorite dogma against the teachings of God's word, and is very well calculated to lead astray the minds of the unwary. In this case, as in the other, the sophistry does not consist so much in the declaration itself, as in the *application* of it. The declaration has *two sides* to it. And conclusions directly the reverse from those usually drawn from it are the correct conclusions. Suppose a particular dogma, the result of philosophical investigation, or "rational deduction," arrays itself against the plain teachings of God's word. Before any conclusion unfavorable to the doctrine of the Scriptures can be drawn from such a dogma, it must be supported by an amount of evidence *superior* to that which substantiates the divine authenticity of the Scriptures. And this we venture to affirm is a case that never occurred. Therefore, the conclusion, in all such cases, is *against the dogma itself*, and *not* against the particular Scripture doctrine which it opposes. The evidences of the divine authenticity of the Scriptures, especially to the Christian, who, in addition to all the rest, may have the evidence of his own experience, may be considered *absolutely conclusive.* We may admit, then, and we believe, that no one truth can contradict another truth, and that

The revelation in God's *works* cannot contradict the revelation in his word:

But the particular dogma *does* contradict the revelation in his word:

Therefore the particular dogma is *not* the revelation of his works.

Again: God's word is *truth:* but

One truth cannot contradict another truth:

But the particular dogma *does* contradict God's word:

Therefore the particular dogma is *not* the truth.

Let us now apply these principles to the theory under consideration. Are our author's "rational deductions" supported by an amount of evidence *superior* to that which authenticates the Bible? Is it more evident that the God of infinite power and wisdom cannot prevent the particles which compose one human body from ever becoming essential parts of another human body, than that his *word* is *true?* Is it more evident that the God by whom the very hairs of our heads are all numbered, and without whose notice not one is permitted to fall to the ground, cannot collect together again the scattered fragments of the human frame, than that the Bible is a divinely inspired record? Is it more evident that God has no use for our bodies in the future world, than that the Scriptures are authentic? Even our author does not pretend this: for he acknowledges on p. 235 that his rational deductions may be false; while he declares, in another place, that he will yield to no man living in his implicit confidence in the Scriptures. While commenting upon John v, 28, 29, he says: "This passage, as understood in its literal import, does certainly encounter the force of that cumulative mass of evidence, built upon rational and philosophical grounds, which we have arrayed against any statement of the doctrine which would imply the participation of the body in that rising again which is predicated of the dead. We do not by any means affirm that the conclusions from that source to which we have come are sufficient of themselves to countervail the rebutting conclusions which may be formed from this text. All we would say is, that they have *weight*, and consequently we are not at liberty at once to dismiss them." P. 235.

Mark this concession. What then is the correct conclusion even from his own premises? Why that his "rational and philosophical deductions," being opposed to the Scriptures, and being supported by evidence vastly less conclusive than that which authenticates the Scriptures, are *themselves irrational, unphilosophical, and false.* Thus in his haste to thrust at the sublime doctrine of the resurrection, he has seized the sword of truth by the *blade*, which, when drawn to give the blow, has *pierced himself.* What then can be the use of all this flourish and parade about "rational and philosophical deductions," as doing away the resurrection of the body, unless it be to entangle and bewilder the unwary, or to captivate those whose empty heads will echc the *sound* philosophy, because nothing but the sound is in *their* heads?

Having wrested, as we claim, the weapon from our opponent, we propose now to use it for a moment ourselves. Setting out then with the proposition, that no one truth can contradict another truth, we say that it is obligatory on him who broaches a new theory whose principles conflict with established truths, to make his theory yield to those truths, and not the truths to his theory. Instead of making his new theory, as Professor B. has done, the "criterion" by which the meaning of the "established truths" is to be known, he is to make the established truths the criterion by which the truthfulness of his new theory is to be tested, bearing in mind that the truths with which the new theory is to be compared must be embraced in the same general subject with the theory itself. For example: The truths of geometry, or electro-magnetism, cannot either favor or oppose the new doctrine of the resurrection, but the truths of revelation, especially upon the subject of the resurrection, can. Tried by these principles, the new doctrine of the resurrection is annihilated at once.

From what has now been said, it is evident that a theory, claiming to be a science perfectly independent of all other sciences, stands or falls according to its own intrinsic merits, without any reference whatever to established truths on other subjects, inasmuch as it is not of a character to be tested by them. Such we claim to be the *Scriptural* theory of the resurrection of the human body. The Scripture doctrine on this subject is, that the resurrection is an effect produced by the immediate agency of God; that it is a miraculous interposition of divine power. Consequently we may admit that the ordinary laws of nature are not sufficient for the accomplishment of such a result, without in the least degree weakening the argument in its favor. The subject, therefore, of the resurrection belonging to the science of *miracles*, must be studied in the *light* of miracles, and in no other light. For the science of miracles is above all other sciences, and independent of them. But a miracle being the result of the immediate agency of divine power, *above* the laws of nature, nothing can prevent its accomplishment, if God intends to perform it, but what limits the divine power. But what can limit the divine power? It can accomplish anything which is not in itself *absurd*, and this is *no* limitation. For example: to say that God cannot make a full grown man of thirty years of age in a moment, is no limitation of divine power, for the proposition is *self-contradictory*. But that God intends to "raise the dead," in the common acceptation of the term *resurrection*, and in the sense in which the *apostles understood* the term, even by the admission of our author, Professor Bush himself would be willing to admit but for his "rational deductions." But I trust it has been shown that these deductions are anything else than "rational." And to say that God ever intended to raise the dead in this sense, and yet that the thing itself is *contradictory* in the nature of the case, is to cast a reflection upon the divine wisdom. Did not God, when he intended it, perfectly understand all the possible contingencies of matter?

But I am willing to enter into a more particular examination of these "rational deductions," by which it is attempted to be shown that the common opinion of the resurrection involves an absurdity, in the nature of the case. Our *opponents affirm*, and *we deny*.

The arguments, from "reason," against the resurrection of the body, may be summed up under four heads.

1. That the body is in a constant state of change, from birth to death; so that when it is said the body shall be raised, it cannot be known *what body* is meant; as the individual, if he be an aged person, has had several entire bodies during lifetime: and if any one of these bodies should be raised, it would not be the body in-

habited by the soul, except for a very small period of human life.

2. That the body becomes totally decomposed after death, mingling with other elements, forming various and numberless new combinations. That parts of it pass away into impalpable gasses; and these again uniting with other substances, and these substances again suffering decomposition, and so on, till the identity of the body is utterly destroyed; so that the identical body never can be raised again.

3. That the resurrection of the identical body implies the resurrection of every identical particle of matter of which the body is composed, neither more nor less: but,

4. That this is impossible in the nature of the case, as one body at death becomes parts of other bodies at their death; and, consequently, that two or more souls would claim the same body, or parts of it, in the resurrection.

Now I undertake to say that *not one* of these four propositions, taken as a whole, can be made out. To begin, then, with the first. There is no doubt but that *some* parts of the human body are in a state of flux, or change; but it is not so evident that *all* the parts are; no man on earth knows it, or *can* know it. But whether the whole body does thus change or not is perfectly immaterial to the argument, so far as the resurrection is concerned; for the Scripture doctrine is, that it is the body that *dies* that is raised again, whether that body "sleeps in the grave," or "in the dust of the earth" elsewhere, or "in the sea." So that if we have had a *hundred* bodies during lifetime, the case is not altered. The last part of this proposition is sufficiently answered by Mr. Watson: "Rewards and punishments have their relation to the body, not so much as it is the *subject*, but the *instrument* of rewards and punishments." As it is the soul only which is the responsible agent, so "it is the soul only which perceives pain or pleasure, which suffers or enjoys, and is, therefore, the only rewardable subject. Were we to admit such corporeal mutations as are assumed in the objection, they affect not the case of our accountability. The personal identity or sameness of a rational being, as says Mr. Locke, consists in self-consciousness. 'By this every one is to himself what he calls *self*, without considering whether that self be continued in the same or diverse substances. It was by the same *self* which reflects upon an action done many years ago that the action was performed.'" But the objection contradicts the common sense of all mankind. Suppose the criminal, who has been sentenced to the penitentiary for fourteen years, should demand his release at the end of seven, on the grounds that it was another body which was sent there seven years before; that they were other hands upon which the chains had been fixed; and, as proof of this, should gravely enumerate the times he had pared his nails, and shaved his beard, since he was sent there; who would think his reasons sufficient to release him, unless for the purpose of sending him from prison to a lunatic asylum?

The second proposition assumes that by reason of the total decomposition, and dispersion, and new compositions and decompositions, taking place with a dead body, that it is not possible that the same identical body can ever be raised again. But why not? Cannot the chemist take a piece of gold coin into his laboratory, file it to powder, dissolve it with acids, alloy it with other metals, grind it again to powder, throw it into the fire, and mingle it with soot, ashes, and charcoal, and yet bring out the same fine gold? And cannot he mold it again in the same die, and be perfectly sure that it is the very same gold? And is the God of all power and wisdom, whose vast laboratory is the *universe*, less skillful than the creatures he has made? And cannot *he*, who is intimately present to every particle of matter, who knows every particle by *name*, and whose power has brought every particle into *being*, collect together again the scattered fragments of the human frame, although mingled with the elements, and driven to the four winds of heaven? May we not reply to those making this objection to the resurrection of the body, "Ye do err, not knowing the Scriptures, nor the *power of God?*"

The third proposition, namely, that which affirms that there can be no resurrection of the identical body, without the resurrection of every particle of gross matter composing the body, has no relevancy to the argument, except by connecting it with the fourth proposition: for unless it can be proved that the very same matter, at least a portion of it, which was possessed by one human body at death, was also possessed by another human body at death, no argument can be drawn from this position unfavorable to the doctrine. It may be observed in this place, however, that those who adopt the commonly received opinion do not contend that just the same amount of gross matter, neither more nor less, which was deposited in the grave, is essential to the resurrection. But they do believe that that which constitutes the essential identity or sameness of the body shall be raised again, not indeed in gross matter, but refined, purified, and made glorious. Our bodies, during lifetime, may vary very considerably, so far as the amount of gross matter contained in them is concerned, and that, too, in a very short space of time; but who supposes that the essential identity of the body is destroyed by this? The proposition contains a fallacy, by putting more into the definition of the word *identity* than the opposite doctrine allows; and then drawing unfavorable conclusions from such definition. This is contrary to all the rules of honorable controversy. But it is contended by Professor Bush, that the very nature of identity absolutely requires all that is put into the definition. But this is not the question. It is enough that his *opponents* do not so *understand* it. The question is not whether the believers in the doctrine of a resurrection have used a particular word in a greater or less extension of meaning than that which rigidly belongs to it, but whether the idea they would convey by it, as explained by themselves, is correct. The dispute is not about the meaning of a *word*, but the reality of a thing. If our author had considered this, he might have saved himself the labor he has bestowed on the subject of identity.

Having encountered nothing formidable in

the first three arguments, let us now examine the fourth. This asserts that in consequence of one body after death becoming parts of other bodies at their death, it is impossible, in the nature of the case, that the same bodies that die should be united again with the same souls with which they have lived: as where human bodies have been decomposed, and their substance gone to support vegetation, and this vegetation nourished other animals, and these animals again gone to the nourishment of man; or, where the human body has gone to the support of grain, and this grain gone to the support of other human beings; or, more directly, where one human being has consumed the flesh of another, as in cannibalism. We have stated the case in all its strength, and are now prepared to look it full in the face.

In regard to the first part of this position, namely, where the decomposed body goes to the support of vegetation, and this vegetation goes to the nourishment of human beings, it may be remarked, that but a small part of earth actually becomes part of vegetation at all. This is demonstrated by the growth of plants and trees, where the entire amount of earth to which their roots had access has been weighed, both before and after their growth. In this manner plants and trees have increased many pounds in weight, while the earth to which their roots had access has diminished but a few ounces; showing that the atmosphere and water contribute very largely to the growth of vegetation. Now, suppose a human being to have eaten grain that had grown upon soil enriched by the decomposition of a human body: allow that he has consumed *one hundred pounds* of such grain; not more than one part in twenty-five of this grain ever becomes actually a part of the human body, that is, four pounds. But not more than one part in twenty of the grain is converted earth, that is, one-fifth of a pound. But probably not more than one part in a *thousand*, to which the roots of the grain had access, was human dust, which, by the previous calculation, would give to the second human body but one part in five thousand of a single pound, that is, the one three hundred and twelfth part of an ounce of matter which had ever been possessed by another human being; and even this small fraction of an ounce might go to the grosser parts of the system, not at all necessary to the resurrection body. And where an animal has intervened, the ratio is immensely diminished.

Again: but a small part of the vegetation concerned in the growth of grain is actually grain itself; and how easy for God, who is not inattentive to anything he has made, and who has adapted means to ends, with infinite skill, throughout every part of nature, to have so ordered, in his providence, that this small part of human dust that actually becomes part of vegetation should lodge in the *roots*, and *stalk*, and leaves, without ever becoming a part of the grain at all! I say, cannot HE DO IT? And is there *any contradiction in terms* here? And remember the question here is, whether the doctrine implies anything which is palpably absurd. If it be said that nothing short of divine interposition can bring out these results, we grant it. But nothing short of divine interposition can effect the resurrection of the body. The same power that can do the one can do the other. Then "why should it be thought incredible," with any who believe in a God of infinite power and wisdom, "that God should raise the dead?"

But let us take the case of cannibalism itself. Now, no considerable portion of the sustenance of any human being has been human flesh. But a small fraction of the entire food, even of those who occasionally indulge in this dreadful practice, has been of this kind. And but a small fraction, even of this small fraction, ever becomes part of the human body, allowing, for the present, that the flesh of one human being may become part of another human being. And even this small fraction may go to the grosser parts of the system, not at all necessary to the resurrection body. So that there is nothing absurd, even here, in the commonly received doctrine of the resurrection. But I have a more weighty argument to offer against this position. We have already seen that the resurrection of the body, belonging to the nature of miracles, must be studied in the *light* of miracles. The question, then, is simply this: If the God of infinite power and wisdom set himself to the accomplishment of this work, can he perform it? We unhesitatingly answer *yes*, and without any contradiction in terms either. To say that the thing is absurd, if we admit that God has set himself to accomplish it, is, as we have already seen, an impeachment of his wisdom. But it may be said, "This is the very thing we deny, namely, that God *has* set himself to the accomplishment of this work." But let it be remembered that it is admitted on all sides that this is the obvious meaning of the Scriptures; and a meaning which all would receive, but for these "rational deductions" which we are now examining, and which alledge that the thing is absurd and self-contradictory. I say, then, we have a right to repeat the inquiry, "If the God of infinite power set himself to accomplish this work, cannot he perform it?" and to answer, as above, He may so order, in his providence, that no human being at death shall possess a single particle of another human being at death, even allowing cannibalism to be ever so much practiced. There are many ways of which *we* can conceive in which this can be done, and no doubt many more are open to the view of infinite wisdom. This may most easily be accomplished by controlling the circumstances of the death of those who have been guilty of this inhuman practice; and by other methods which have already been enumerated, even upon the supposition that one part of a human body may become, at some period, a portion of another body.

But we will now admit, for the sake of the argument, what is claimed in the third proposition, that the resurrection of the identical body requires the resurrection of all the gross materials of which the body is composed; not indeed in gross materials; and *then* show that the doctrine implies nothing contradictory or absurd. For then, examining the subject in the light of miracles, we have only to consider the Supreme

Being as undertaking the task of raising every human body, *entire*, as it respects the amount of matter possessed by it at death. And is it not infinitely easy for Him so to order, in his power and wisdom, that no part of one human body after death shall ever become a part of another human body, under any circumstances? Is it not as easy that a law shall be stamped upon the matter composing the human body, by which it cannot become amalgamated with another human body, as that a similar law should exist in regard to *oil* and *water*, or *iron* and *clay*? And cannot He who could cause *five loaves* and *two fishes* to nourish *five thousand men*, besides *women and children*, also cause the other food that has been eaten to be entirely sufficient for the nourishment of the human body, no matter how much the practice to which we have alluded has prevailed? And would he not *do* it before his ultimate purpose in this respect should be thwarted? Are the divine resources so *feeble* and scanty; are the ultimate designs of the eternal Jehovah so circumscribed, that a mere pigmy can throw them into confusion? "Well, but this could not be done without a miracle." Well, what then? The whole subject of the resurrection belongs to miracles. Why will men, professing to believe the Bible, identify themselves with rationalists and infidels, in their abhorrence of anything miraculous? Who shall stand up to "limit the Holy One of Israel?" We have seen, then, that this last and most plausible objection interposes no serious obstacle in the way of the sublime and *Scriptural* doctrine of the resurrection of the body.

The opposing theory is built upon doubtful deductions drawn from doubtful hypotheses?

I have bestowed the more attention upon these positions, because they contain the whole strength of the argument against the resurrection of the body. It is admitted that the plain letter of inspiration teaches another doctrine. "But this doctrine," it is said, "encounters insuperable difficulties." So then, if these "insuperable difficulties" have been fairly removed, the argument is yielded at once; inasmuch as these "difficulties" are all that have prevented the Scriptural doctrine from being received.

All that is claimed, however, in this humble effort thus far, is, that the doctrine has been rescued from the bewilderments of a vain philosophy, and placed where we may contemplate it in the brighter and purer light of divine inspiration. Indeed, I suppose that an appeal directly to the *Scriptures*, without this tedious examination of our author's "rational deductions," would have been all-sufficient with most who have listened to these remarks; but it is not so with all. And to many it will afford a higher degree of *satisfaction*, if not a higher degree of evidence, to know that these philosophical objections are themselves *unphilosophical.*

The light of the sun may be obscured by fogs, and mists, and clouds; so may the light of revelation by the bewildering speculations of a pseudo philosophy. You are well aware, my brethren, of the effect upon the youthful mind of an array of the high-sounding titles, "reason," "science," and "philosophy," when an attempt to array them is made, as in the present case, against the Scriptures. To rescue one youthful spirit who might be just upon the outer current of the maelstrom, whose constant influence, "drawing inward and downward," is to swallow up, and engulf him in ruin, were an undertaking worthy of an angel—I hope an anxiety of this sort may atone for what might otherwise be somewhat tedious. If one of the feeblest of God's children should find his faith strengthened, or if any lingering skepticism should be dispelled from the mind of any, then shall I not have "labored in vain." Finally, my dear brethren, is there not an elevated satisfaction—a holy enjoyment, when, after following error into its lurking places, descending its dark and winding labyrinths, and traversing its damp, and cloudy, and miry vale, by the aid of the compass, we find ourselves in the clear sunshine, and see that our foundation is the rock?

PART II.

SCRIPTURAL ARGUMENT—THE RESURRECTION OF OUR SAVIOUR CONSIDERED.

Why should it be thought a thing incredible with you that God should raise the dead?—Acts xxvi, 8.

HAVING shown, in the preceding remarks, that the argument from the "light of reason," against the resurrection of the body, interposes no serious obstacle in the way of the doctrine, but is itself most unreasonable, we are now ready to pursue the subject in the clearer light of revelation.

As Jesus Christ in his human nature was the first that rose from the dead to die no more, and as his resurrection is both a pledge and a sample of the resurrection of believers, it will be our object in the present discourse to examine the nature of his resurrection.

Let it be borne in mind that the author, whose book has been the occasion of this discourse, asserts that all the resurrection there is for a human being "is simply a state of future existence or immortality." That "the disengagement of the spiritual body takes place at the *moment of death*." That this principle, the spiritual body—by which he evidently means what is commonly understood by the soul—"*lives* again, because it *never* dies." And that this *is all the resurrection our Saviour ever experienced.* That all that ever did rise of Jesus Christ, arose at the moment of his death!!

Truly a new turn has been given to the controversy respecting the resurrection of our Lord. The fact of his resurrection has been demonstrated over and over again, with the clearness of a sunbeam, when assailed by the scoffs and sneers of infidelity. But latterly a "new invention" has been "wrought out"—a new species of infidelity has sprung up, which admits all the evidence in favor of the fact, and yet denies the fact itself; with how much propriety, I trust the present discourse will show. Whatever becomes of the author of this new theory, I cannot but believe, it would have been better for the world if the *theory* "had never been born."

But "to the law and the testimony." David prophesied of Christ's resurrection in the following words: "My *flesh* also shall rest in hope, for thou wilt not leave my soul in hell; neither wilt thou suffer thy Holy One to see corruption." Psa. xvi, 9, 10. Upon this passage the apostle Peter makes the following comment: (Acts ii, 25–35)—"For David speaketh concerning him, I foresaw the Lord always before my face;

for he is on my right hand, that I should not be moved: therefore did my heart rejoice, and my tongue was glad; moreover also, my flesh shall rest in hope: because thou wilt not leave my soul in hell, neither wilt thou suffer thy Holy One to see corruption. Thou hast made known to me the ways of life; thou shalt make me full of joy with thy countenance. Men and brethren, let me freely speak unto you of the patriarch David, that he is both dead and buried, and his sepulchre is with us unto this day. Therefore being a prophet, and knowing that God had sworn with an oath to him, that of the fruit of his loins, according to the flesh, he would raise Christ to sit on his throne; he, seeing this before, spake of the resurrection of Christ, that his soul was not left in hell, neither his flesh did see corruption. This Jesus hath God raised up, whereof we all are witnesses. Therefore being by the right hand of God exalted, and having received of the Father the promise of the Holy Ghost, he hath shed forth this, which ye now see and hear. For David is not ascended into the heavens: but he saith himself, The Lord said unto my lord, Sit thou on my right hand, until I make thy foes thy footstool."

Thus it is seen, that St. Peter applies this passage in Psalms to the resurrection of Christ.

But how could the declaration, "My flesh shall rest in hope," be a prophecy of his resurrection, if his flesh had mingled with the elements, as is contended for by Professor B., and his body never be raised from the dead? And how could the declaration, "Neither wilt thou suffer thy Holy One to see corruption," be a prophecy of Christ's resurrection, unless it was spoken of his body? For in the soul there is no tendency to corruption. The spiritual body of the new theory "lives again in a future state *because* it never dies." It is essentially immortal and incorruptible according to the theory itself. But Peter, in order to convince the Jews, who, it would seem, applied this prophecy to David himself, that they were mistaken, and that it applied to Christ, and not to David, says that "David is both dead and buried, and his sepulchre is with us to this day." And again, verse 34, "For David is not ascended into the heavens." But David's *soul* had been in heaven for *centuries*. It is as plain as anything can be, that Peter speaks of David's *body*, which had not yet ascended to heaven, in contradistinction from *Christ's body* which *had* ascended to heaven.

St. Paul quotes the same passage from the Psalms for the very same object, namely, to convince the Jews that Jesus had risen from the dead, according to the *Scriptures*. The following is the quotation by the apostle Paul, together with his comment upon the passage: (Acts xiii, 34–37)—"And as concerning that he raised him up from the dead, now no more to return to corruption, he said on this wise, I will give you the sure mercies of David. Wherefore he saith also in another psalm, Thou shalt not suffer thy Holy One to see corruption. For David, after he had served his own generation by the will of God, fell on sleep, and was laid unto his fathers, and *saw* corruption: but he whom God raised again, saw no corruption."

This explanation perfectly harmonizes with that of Peter, together with the positive declaration that David saw corruption in consequence of death in opposition to Christ, who saw no corruption.

Can anything possibly be plainer from the explanation of these apostles, both of whom quote this psalm to prove the resurrection of Christ, that the *body* of David had suffered corruption, or *decomposition*, in consequence of death, while Christ's *body* had been raised before any corruption or decomposition had taken place? But how, it may be asked, does the new theory escape these conclusions? I answer,

It cannot escape them. All it attempts to do is to prove, what no one denies, that these passages "allude exclusively to the resurrection of Christ." Very well: they allude expressly to the resurrection of Christ; and this is the very purpose for which we have here introduced them. Where is the force of the argument of the apostles to convince the Jews, from their *own scriptures*, that Jesus had risen from the dead, according to our author's theory? This theory maintains, that all that ever rose of our Saviour, rose at the very moment of death, and that "his body was miraculously resolved into its primitive elements, while laying in the tomb of Joseph!!" Pages 166, 167. In the light, or rather *darkness*, of this new theory, let us look at the argument of the apostles, to show that David was not speaking of *himself*, but of Christ. 1st. David was dead; well, so was Christ. 2d. David's sepulchre was with them; so was Christ's. 3d. But David had not yet ascended to heaven. This cannot mean his *spiritual* body: for this, according to the theory, "rose at the very moment of his death." It "was exhaled with the dying breath." Then it must mean his *natural* body had not ascended to heaven; so neither had Christ's. 4th. But David fell asleep in death, and saw corruption in consequence of death; so also did Christ, with only this difference, that while David's body was suffered to see corruption by the ordinary process of decomposition, our Saviour's body did not see corruption, by the *extraordinary* process of a miracle! What an overwhelming argument to the Jew!!

The new theory will have to undergo a long process of "progressive improvement," before its application to these passages will make anything but ridiculous nonsense. But Christ himself foretold the nature and time of his own resurrection. Let us now examine his own prophesies in relation to this event, and see how they agree with the notion that a spiritual body was developed at the moment of death, and that his natural body never rose at all. In Matthew xvi, 21, we have his prophecy, as follows: "From that time forth began Jesus to show unto his disciples, how that he must go unto Jerusalem, and suffer many things of the elders and chief priests, and scribes, and be killed, and be raised again the third day." See also the parallel passages in the other evangelists. From this it is manifest that he made his death and resurrection a subject of frequent conversation. "From that time forth began Jesus to show unto his disciples," &c. Accordingly, a short time after this, we have a repetition of the same prophecy, as follows: (Matt. xx, 17–19)—"And Jesus going up to Jerusalem, took the twelve disciples apart in the way, and said unto them, Behold, we go up to Jerusalem; and the Son of man shall be betrayed unto the chief priests, and unto the scribes, and they shall condemn him to death, and shall deliver him to the Gentiles to mock, and to scourge, and to crucify him: and the *third* day he shall rise again." The theory teaches expressly, that all the resurrection our Saviour ever experienced was at the moment of death; but Christ himself declares, that he should rise on the *third day*. One declaration or the other must be false: for they flatly contradict each other. *Something* was to be raised the third day. What was it? It was not his soul, for this did not die. It was not such a spiritual body as the new theory contends for, for by the theory itself, such a body is essentially immortal, and "lives in a future state, *because it never dies*," and is developed at the moment of death. What then *was* it? It was something that was to be *crucified*—something that was to be *killed*. What was it that was to be *crucified* and *killed?* The body, and nothing but the body. And the *body*, and nothing but the *body*, was to rise again on the third day. Otherwise, how is there any meaning at all in the language?

Take another declaration of our Saviour respecting this event: (John ii, 18–22)—"Then answered the Jews, and said unto him, What sign showest thou unto us, seeing thou doest these things? Jesus answered and said unto them, Destroy this temple, and in three days I will raise it up. Then said the Jews, Forty and six years was this temple in building, and wilt thou rear it up in three days? But he spake of the temple of his *body*. When, therefore, he was risen from the dead, his disciples remembered that he said this unto them; and they believed the Scriptures, and the word which Jesus had said." Mark the language of verse twenty-one, "But he spake of the temple of his *body*." What else could the Jews *destroy?* They could destroy his body, that is, they could kill his body, and nothing but his body; and the same body which the Jews could, and would destroy, he would raise up in three days after.

Let us now see how the *event fulfilled* these prophecies: (Luke xxiv, 1–8)—"Now, upon the first day of the week, very early in the morning, they came unto the sepulchre, bringing the spices which they had prepared, and certain others with them. And they found the stone rolled away from the sepulchre. And they entered in, and found not the body of the Lord Jesus. And it came to pass, as they were much perplexed thereabout, behold, two men stood by them in shining garments: and as they were afraid, and bowed down their faces to the earth, they said unto them, Why seek ye the living among the dead? He is not here, but is risen: remember how he spake unto you when he was yet in Galilee, saying, The Son of man must be delivered into the hands of sinful men, and be crucified, and the third day rise again. And they remembered his words." Now let it be remembered that these females, having prepared spices and ointments for the body of Jesus on *Friday*, and rested on the sabbath, (Luke xxiii, 56,) came very early to the sepulchre, on Sunday morning, with the spices which they had prepared for the purpose of anointing the *body* of Jesus. "And when they found not the *body* of Jesus, they were much perplexed thereabout." About not finding the *body* of Jesus in the sepulchre. In the midst of their grief and perplexity, two angels appeared in shining garments, and declared that he was not there, but had risen as he had said he should. Now, what did they expect to find in the tomb of Joseph? Not his *spirit* certainly. They had witnessed his expiring agony upon the cross; they had heard him commend his spirit into the hands of God; they had witnessed his giving up the ghost; they had seen the Roman soldier, with a heart as hard as the steel in his weapon, thrust a spear deep into the side of the innocent Redeemer, after he was already dead; they had taken particular notice of the manner in which his lifeless body had been laid in the tomb three days before. Luke xxiii, 55.

What, I ask again, did they expect *to find* in the sepulchre? Why the *body*, and nothing but the *body*. And therefore the answer of the angels could not have meant anything else than that his body, his *natural body*, had risen again.

In Matthew's account of his resurrection we have some additional particulars: (Matt. xxviii, 1–9)—"In the end of the sabbath, as it began to dawn toward the first day of the week, came Mary Magdalene, and the other Mary, to see the sepulchre. And behold, there was a great earthquake: for the angel of the Lord descended from heaven, and came and rolled back the stone from the door, and sat upon it. His countenance was like lightning, and his raiment white as snow: and for fear of him the keepers did shake, and became as dead men. And the angel answered and said unto the women, Fear not ye: for I know that ye seek Jesus, which was crucified. He is not here; for he is risen, as he said. Come, see the place where the Lord lay: and go quickly, and tell his disciples that he is risen from the dead; and behold, he goeth before you into Galilee; there shall ye see him: lo, I have told you. And they departed quickly from the sepulchre with fear and great joy, and did run to bring his disciples word. And as they went to tell his disciples, behold, Jesus met them, saying, All hail. And they came and held him by the feet, and worshiped him." Look at the reason which the angel gives why the body of Jesus is not there: "He is not here; *for* (or *because*) he is risen, as he said." But when had Jesus ever *said* a word about a spiritual body *emerging at the moment of death?* Professor B. talks about this, but our Saviour never. But how does the angel propose to convince these persons that the body was not yet in the tomb? Why by inviting them to "come and see the *place* where the *Lord lay.*" Now *what* had lain in the tomb? Why the *body* of Jesus: and the reason why it was not there when these persons came, the angel affirms, was that he had risen again. Can anything be plainer, than that the angel of the Lord, who had previously descended and rolled away the stone from the door of the sepulchre, *intended* that these females should understand that the real body of Jesus had risen from the dead? But look at another item in this history. When these females, overwhelmed with astonishment, ran, with fear and great joy, to publish these things to the disciples, Jesus met them on their way, and exclaimed, All hail. What follows? And they came and held him by the *feet*, and worshiped him. If it is *true* that they held Jesus by the feet, then had his *body* risen again. If the new theory is true, then this passage is *not* true. Those who believe the *Bible* will not hesitate in this matter. In Luke xxiv, 33–44, we have an account of what transpired between Christ and his disciples, in Jerusalem, the night after his resurrection. After two of the disciples of Christ, though not apostles, had been to a village, called Emmaus, and had seen our Saviour, and he had made known himself to them in the breaking of bread, "they rose up the same hour, and returned to Jerusalem, and found the eleven gathered together, and them that were with them, saying, The Lord is risen indeed, and hath appeared to Simon. And they told what things were done in the way, and how he was known of them in breaking of bread. And as they thus spake, Jesus himself stood in the midst of them, and saith unto them, Peace be unto you. But they were terrified and affrighted, and supposed that they had seen a spirit. And he said unto them, Why are ye troubled? and why do thoughts arise in your hearts? Behold my *hands* and my *feet*, that it is I myself: handle me, and see; for a spirit hath not flesh and bones, as ye see me have. And when he had thus spoken, he showed them his hands and his feet. And while they yet believed not for joy, and wondered, he said unto them, Have ye here any meat? And they gave him a piece of a broiled fish, and of a honeycomb. And he took it, and did eat before them. And he said unto them, These are the words which I spake unto you, while I was yet with you, that all things must be fulfilled which were written in the law of Moses, and in the prophets, and in the Psalms, concerning me."

In the history of the same event, as recorded by St. John, we have the additional item of information relative to Thomas, who was not present with the other apostles, at their first interview with the risen Saviour: (John xx, 24–28) —"But Thomas, one of the twelve, called Didymus, was not with them when Jesus came.

The other disciples therefore said unto him, We have seen the Lord. But he said unto them, Except I shall see in his hands the print of the nails, and put my finger into the print of the nails, and thrust my hand into his side, I will not believe. And after eight days, again his disciples were within, and Thomas with them. Then came Jesus, the doors being shut, and stood in the midst, and said, Peace be unto you. Then saith he to Thomas, Reach hither thy finger, and behold my hands; and reach hither thy hand, and thrust it into my side: and be not faithless, but believing. And Thomas answered and said unto him, My Lord and my God."

In our examination of the preceding scriptures, it appeared most evident, that the angel of the Lord intended that those who came early to the sepulchre should believe that the real human body of our Saviour had risen from the dead. In the passages now under consideration it is equally evident that our Saviour *himself* intended that the disciples should believe that his veritable body had risen. His disciples had been his daily and familiar companions for more than three years. They were familiar with his countenance, with his voice, and with all the circumstances of his person. Probably there was no person upon earth whom they could identify with more unerring certainty. But yet his sudden and unexpected appearance among them, when the "doors were shut" at night, excited their fears, and they supposed they had seen a *spirit*. But, after calming their fears, and soothing that perturbation of spirit which his sudden appearance among them had occasioned, he then appeals to their own *senses* in proof of the resurrection of his real body: "Feel me, and see that it is I myself: *handle* me, and see; for a spirit hath *not flesh and bones, as ye see me have*." He then showed them his hands and his feet. Did he not intend by this, that they should understand that his human body had risen again? For what other purpose did he require them to handle him? For what other purpose did he show them his own hands and feet? For what other purpose did he declare that a spirit had not flesh and bones as *he* had, and as they *saw* him have? Was it *true* that our Saviour's resurrection body possessed "flesh and bones?" Was it *true* that he showed them his hands, his *real hands*, and feet? Is it *true* that they *saw*, and felt, and knew that he had flesh and bones, and hands and feet, after his resurrection? To say they did *not know* this, is to accuse our

Saviour with *falsehood*. To say they *did know* it, is to ruin the new theory. Who but an infidel can hesitate, for a moment, what course to take? I would not say that the author of the new theory is an infidel, so far as to deny the Scriptures as a whole; but on this particular doctrine his views are infidel to all intents and purposes. But our Saviour went still further in his design to convince the disciples that his body had risen: he *ate* in their presence. And, in the midst of these demonstrations of his real resurrection, our Saviour says to the disciples: "These are the words which I spake unto you, while I was yet with you, that all things must be fulfilled which were written in the law of Moses, and in the prophets, and in the Psalms, concerning me." Luke xxiv, 44. Now one of these things which was "written in the Psalms concerning him" was that his *flesh* should rest in *hope*, and his body should not see corruption.

But Thomas was not present on this occasion; and, when the other disciples related to him what they had seen, it seeemed to him "incredible;" and he declared he would not believe it, unless he should put his fingers into the prints of the nails, and thrust his hand into his side that had been pierced by the soldier's spear. Is it not perfectly evident from this, that Thomas understood the other disciples to affirm that the real body of Christ had risen from the dead? Why else should he speak of the "prints in his hands," and of his side that had been pierced? The conclusion is irresistible. Bearing this in mind, mark what follows. Eight days after this, the disciples were again together, under circumstances very much like those of their first meeting, the "doors being shut," and Thomas was with them. And now Jesus appeared in the midst of them, as at the first time; and, addressing *Thomas*, says, "Reach hither thy finger, and put it into the *prints of the nails;* and reach forth thy hand, and *thrust it into my side:* and be not faithless, but believing." Our Saviour knew that Thomas had avowed that he would not be satisfied without this test; and he appeals to this test itself. Thomas had understood the disciples to affirm that Christ's natural body had arisen. This he disbelieved, unless he should have evidence of a particular character. Our Saviour furnished the identical evidence he had called for; and then tells him to be no longer faithless, but believing. Is it not as clear as the light of the sun, that our Saviour *intended* to convince Thomas that the very same body that had hung upon the cross, the very same hands and feet that had been nailed to the wood, the very same side that had been pierced with a spear, had risen again? The evidence is absolutely conclusive to any *sane* mind.

The advocates of the new theory are driven, then, *irresistibly*, to one of two conclusions: *either to accuse the Saviour of the world with deliberate falsehood*, or RENOUNCE *their theory*.

And our Saviour's *intention*, in regard to Thomas, had the *desired* effect; for, while Thomas gazed upon the well-known countenance of his Master, and listened to his *familiar* voice, and saw that look of mingled reproof and compassionate kindness, without, I imagine, waiting to thrust his hand into his side, he rushes to the embrace of his Redeemer, and exclaims, "My Lord and my God."

Professor Bush says of the resurrection body of his theory, p. 70, "We may not be able to *see* it, to *handle* it, to *analyze*, or *describe* it, * * * * it lives again in a future state, *because* it never dies." But Christ's resurrection body *could be "seen," "felt," "analyzed,"* and "*described;*" and it was both *dead* and *buried*, and "lives again, *because* it" has *risen from the dead*, and *not* because it never died. Therefore, the resurrection body of our Saviour is *not* the resurrection body of the new theory; consequently, the theory is *false*, so far as its application to this case is concerned.

But there is yet another class of scriptures which ruins this modern doctrine of the resurrection. I allude to those which represent Christ as the *first* that should rise from the dead. In Revelation i, 5, he is called "the *first begotten* of the dead." In 1 Cor. xv, 20, he is called the "*first fruits*" of the resurrection. Both of these passages most evidently mean that Christ was the *first* who rose from the dead; that is, who rose *immortal*. But in Acts xxvi, 23, it is declared expressly, that he was the first that should rise from the dead. How could it be true, by the new theory, that Christ was the *first* to rise from the dead, if the resurrection body is developed at the moment of death, and "is simply a future state or immortality?" Men had been rising, in this sense, according to the theory itself, for four thousand years.

I have not adduced all the Scripture testimony on this subject of Christ's resurrection which might have been brought; but if what has already been adduced fail of establishing the truth of a literal resurrection of our Saviour's material body, we may despair of proving anything by testimony.

Let us now see how this mass of cumulative evidence is disposed of by our author.

1st. "It is nowhere *expressly* affirmed in Scripture that the *identical material* body of Christ arose." P. 152.

We answer, it is nowhere expressly affirmed in Scripture that our Saviour *had* any "identical material body;" nor that anybody else ever "had any identical material body." Indeed, neither the word "identical" nor "material" occurs anywhere in the "Scriptures," in *any* connection whatever. Why not deny, then, that our Saviour, or anybody else, ever had any "identical material body?" There is the very same evidence that our Saviour's identical material body rose from the dead, that we have to prove that he had any "identical material body" at all: *the very same.*

May we not expect, that in the subsequent progressive improvements of this new theory it will be denied that our Saviour *had any material body?* The system will then have the merit of being consistent with itself, at least; and that is certainly much more than it can claim, with any show of truth, at the present stage of development.

But we affirm, and are ready to stake our reputation upon the *issue*, that the *evidence is even stronger from Scripture to prove the literal resurrection of our Saviour's body*, than it would have been had the expression "identical material body" been substituted for the expressions actually employed. These Scriptural expressions constitute what logicians call *a real* definition—a definition *of a thing* by *enumerating the principal attributes* of that thing. Thus, the body of our Saviour, which rose from the dead, according to the Scriptures, was the body which had been "killed" by being "crucified;" the body which had "hands," and "feet," and "side," which "hands," and "feet," and "side," *still* bore the prints of the nails and spear which had pierced them while hanging upon the cross. This definition is *more specific*, as every man of Professor Bush's celebrity knows, or *ought* to know, than merely the expression, "identical material body."

2d. "It seems to be a fair presumption, that the same body which rose, also ascended. But the evidence is certainly conclusive, that it was not a material body which ascended to heaven." P. 153. Pray where is this "conclusive evidence" to be found? We *deny* it utterly, and call for the proof. We admit "that the same body which rose also ascended," and conclusions the very reverse of our author's follow inevitably. Our author's argument reduced to form stands thus:

1. The body which rose also ascended.

2. But the body which ascended was not a material body.

3. Therefore the body which rose was not a material body.

Now the professor has not produced a particle of evidence to substantiate the minor proposition, and we challenge him to produce any. The very reverse is positively and unequivocally proved in the Scriptures; consequently his conclusion is *false*.

Let us begin then, as he begins.

1. The body which rose also ascended.

2. But the body which rose has been proved to be material, by the prints of the nails and spear, in the hands, feet, and side.

3. Therefore the body which ascended *was* material.

Logic must undergo a vast "progressive improvement," before it can ever sanction the conclusions of our author.

3d. It is argued that the circumstances connected with our Saviour's appearance to Mary at the sepulchre—to the two disciples on their way to Emmaus—and also to the disciples the following evening, are incompatible with the notion of a material body. Let us see if this objection is any more reasonable than the last.

1. Mary mistook the Saviour for the gardener. From this it is argued that it could not have been his material body which had risen. Now let it be remembered, that she came to the sepulchre "*very early* in the morning," (Luke xxiv, 1,) "as it began to *dawn*, toward the first day of the week," (Matt. xxviii, 1,) but "was yet *dark*." (John xx, 1.) And where is there any difficulty in the case? When it was not sufficiently light, to distinguish one person from another, Mary mistook our Saviour for the gardener!

2. In regard to his appearance to the two disciples as they were going to Emmaus, it is said, "Their eyes were holden that they *should not know him*." Luke xxiv, 16. Our Saviour chose to make himself known to them at the breaking of bread, and in this act their *eyes were opened*, and they knew him. Verse 31. Is there any difficulty in the way of a material body here? Our Lord chose not to make himself known unto them, until their journey was finished, a journey of only a little more than an hour, preferring to do it when they were quietly seated at the table, and on this account their "eyes were holden." Are not these very

flimsy objections to be arrayed against a doctrine supported by such a mass of evidence as we have examined?

3. Let us now examine the circumstances of his appearance among the disciples when the "door was shut." The objection is, that a material body could not suddenly appear in a room having the doors closed and bolted, without a miracle. P. 153. Well, what then? Suppose a miracle was wrought? Was not our Saviour once found walking on the sea in the midst of a dreadful storm? And can a material body walk upon the boisterous waves of the sea without a miracle? What then is the conclusion? Why, according to our author, that our Saviour *never had any material body!!* But he argues in *this very connection*, that our Saviour wrought a miracle in assuming the *appearance* of a material body, with *hands*, and *feet*, and *side*, that had been *pierced*, and *still bore the prints*. And all just for the purpose of making Thomas and the other disciples believe that his material body had risen, when, according to his own theory, no such body had ever risen at all, and concludes, finally, "that a miracle must have been wrought on either view." That is, if his body *was* material, a miracle was wrought in suddenly entering a closed room; and if his body *was not* ma-

terial, or rather if he *had no material* body, a miracle must have been wrought in assuming all the appearances of one. So say we; with just this difference, that by our "view," a miracle was wrought to make the disciples believe the *truth*, and by his "view," a miracle was wrought to make them believe a *falsehood*. For he admits, and even argues, on p. 167, that our Saviour *intended* that the disciples should believe that his material body had risen!! and "that the apostles *believed* the doctrine, and *preached* it," p. 165; that such were their crude conceptions, "that they could not at once come to a sudden recognition of a spiritual presence." However, he thinks that "*subsequently* they *may* have come to entertain more correct notions on the subject." "At all events," says he, "there is no reason why *their* knowledge should be the limit of *ours*." Strange! I wonder what we know about it, except what we have learned from them?

But let us go on and see the measure of absurdity filled to the very *brim*.

4. It is maintained that our Saviour's pretended resurrection on the third day was only "the putting forth of a *visible effect*;" that his showing his hands and his feet to his disciples, as well as his eating in their presence, were

"OPTICAL" "ILLUSIONS." It is true, he does not join these two words together, so as to form the phrase "optical illusions:" but says his showing his hands, &c., were "*optical* acts," pp. 154, 155, and then says, "When we consider the object to be attained by such an *illusion*, we see nothing inconsistent or unworthy the divine impersonification of truth in having recourse to it"!!! P. 155. So then we have the earthquake, the descending of the angel, to roll away the stone from the door of the sepulchre—the announcement of the angels that our Saviour had risen on the third morning, all resolved into a *solemn farce;* the mere "putting forth of a visible effect," and "the appearance" of our Saviour's body still bearing the prints of violence, all resolved into an "*optical*" "*illusion.*" Yea more, and the Saviour of the world *perpetrating* a *deliberate falsehood*, and that too, in regard to the most important event that ever transpired in our world!!! I ask, is not the measure of absurdity full? The God of *eternal truth* joining with *angels* to practice a *pious fraud*—a kind of *miraculous juggling*—a species of *optically miraculous* and *illusive legerdemain!!* Such are the monstrous and abominable absurdities of a system which sets up enfeebled human reason against the plain teachings of God's word. Mr. B. thinks such an "*optical illusion*" is worthy the character of God, "considering the *object* to be attained by it." But what was this *object?* Why to make the disciples and the world believe what was *not true*, that the material body of our Lord had risen from the dead. Such "optical" farcical illusions are worthy the system which has resorted to them, but let them not be charged upon the God of truth. Will our author's notions of "progressive improvement" help him in this extremity? If so, he is desired to tell us, by what progressive improvement in the laws of optics, in the sense of *seeing*, *hearing*, and *feeling*, the stupendous scenes of our Saviour's resurrection, together with many of the *bodies* of the saints which were uncovered by the previous earthquake, and which arose after his resurrection, and went into the holy city and appeared unto many, are all resolved into an "*optical illusion*;" a mere phantasm—an illusive spectral nonentity! And by what "progressive improvement" in the moral character of God has it *now* become consistent for Him who, amid the terrible thunderings of Sinai, said in a voice that shook the earth, Thou shalt *not* lie, to lend the influence of his own lofty example to the most glaring falsehood?

5. It becomes necessary for this system, after

denying that the body of our Lord ever rose from the dead, to tell us what became of it. Well, here you have it: "The body which hung upon the cross was *miraculously* resolved into its primitive elements"!! We shall cease to be astonished hereafter at anything our author shall say. The measure of absurdity already full, is now "pressed down, shaken together, and running over." Why did not the angel say to the distressed disciples, who were perplexed and overwhelmed with grief, at not finding the Saviour's body at the sepulchre, "Behold, he is not here, he has been miraculously dissolved and resolved to his primitive elements;" and not say what was not true, that he had risen again? This, if it had been true, would have been a sufficient reason for his body's not being there. But the angel says, "It is not here, *for*, or *because*, it is *risen* again, as he said." Was a falsehood better than the truth? Our author thinks so, "considering the object to be attained," namely, to make the *disciples* and the *world believe a false doctrine.*

But let us look at this position in the light of the prophecy of David, which prophecy, as we have already seen, both Peter and Paul apply to the resurrection of Christ. Our Saviour is represented as addressing the Father, and saying, "My *flesh* shall rest in hope, for thou wilt not suffer thy Holy One to see corruption." "My flesh shall rest in hope." Hope of what? Why speedy dissolution in the tomb of Joseph. It shall "hope" to be "dissolved, and resolved to its primitive elements," within less than three days after death. And how was the other part of the prophecy fulfilled, namely, "Neither wilt thou suffer thy Holy One to see corruption?" Why, it was not only *not* fulfilled at all, but a miracle was wrought to prevent its fulfillment. He *saw* corruption, and that too so rapidly that it took a *miracle* to accomplish it. If the author of the new doctrine had deliberately set himself to work to get up a system which would destroy all confidence in the Bible, I see not how he could have more effectually answered his purpose. If the apostles, and the world through the apostles, have been *deceived* in the matter of our Saviour's resurrection, who can tell in how many other things they have not been deceived? Well may the pious Christian exclaim in reference to such miserable theories, in the language of weeping Mary, "They have taken away my Lord, and I know not where they have laid him."

If the new theory was a mere matter of opinion, in regard to matters of minor importance, the case would be different. But it strikes at the very heart of the Christian system. It lays the ax at the very root of the tree of life. It seeks to banish from the earth a truth upon which hangs the hope of the world. And such is the tenacity with which it clings to a position once taken, that heaven and earth must give way before it. It robs man of all confidence, either in the *Bible* or the God of the Bible; it is a system which aims a fatal blow at the great and fundamental doctrine of the *atonement, because,* "He that hath ears to hear let him hear;" it sets forth the Saviour of the world as an *impostor,* and the God of eternal truth as *practicing falsehood.* The resurrection of our blessed Lord is truth *too* precious in its character and bearings to be mangled and murdered in this manner. It takes *too* deep a hold upon our deathless interests to be thus fretted away to nothing. The resurrection was the grand crowning miracle in the stupendous scheme of human redemption, and the one upon which our Saviour himself chiefly relied to substantiate his claim as Redeemer of the world. To destroy confidence in this doctrine, therefore, is to unsettle the very foundations of our holy Christianity. All our fondly cherished hopes perish. All our bright prospects are blasted for ever. All our most cherished anticipations are to *realize* only a gloomy wilderness of dreary desolation. What we fondly imagined was the sun shining in his strength, was but the "*illusive*" blaze of the *meteor* whose momentary glow is succeeded by a dark, moonless, starless night, when the chill-dews of despair for ever lower over our future destinies. Is this saying too much? Then hear the apostle Paul: "If Christ be not risen, then is our preaching vain, and your faith is also vain. Yea, and we are found false witnesses of God; because we have testified of God that he raised up Christ: whom he raised not up, if so be that the dead rise not. And if Christ be not raised, your faith is *vain; ye are yet in your sins.* Then they also which are fallen asleep in Christ are *perished.*" 1 Cor. xv, 14, 15, 17, 18.

Verily, we must have something more substantial than *mere appearances* on which to rest our hopes of heaven. Our crimes are too heinous—our depravity is too deep and damning, to be cleansed by such means. Our hearts are too "deceitful and desperately wicked" to be saved by *deceit* and falsehood. The imperishable interests which cluster around the scenes of eternal retribution are too vast and important to be trusted to mere "optical illusions," whose laudable "object" is to *deceive.* I repeat it, *we must have something better.* And blessed be God we *have something better.* "Now *is* Christ risen from the dead, and become the first fruits of them that slept." If our hearts are ready to die within us, when we contemplate the last mysterious agony of our dying Lord, our hearts also leap with overflowing gratitude and joy, when we see him rise again, all glorious and immortal. It is true he suffers the death of a malefactor. The innocent Jesus submits to a wicked and unlawful sentence. He yields his back to the scourges—his temples to the "crown of thorns"—his cheeks to the hand of violence—his hands and feet to be torn by the nails that fasten them to the cross; and all this is nothing compared to the unutterable agony his spirit endures while a world's guilt presses upon him, and like myriads of poisoned arrows pierces his very soul. There he hangs upon the cross: the Creator of the world! his blood flowing down upon his body till it stains all his raiment. There he hangs, bleeding, agonizing, dying; his friends at a little distance weeping, and his enemies insulting and deriding him. When the great purposes of his suffering are accomplished, he cries, "It is finished," and meekly bows his head in death. His enemies now triumph, and his friends give up all for lost. How little do they understand that his death, which for the present blasts all their prospects, is nevertheless the hope of the world!

The sabbath draws near, and his friends, having obtained permission, take down his body from the cross, and carefully inter it in the tomb of Joseph. The sabbath comes, and again all is quiet in Jerusalem. His enemies enjoy a kind of infernal satisfaction in the belief that they have now rid themselves of one whose holy life and pointed reproofs exposed their own moral deformity. They are now confident that they have seen an end of the obnoxious Nazarene, and shall soon see an end of the despised sect of his followers. His friends, alarmed for their own safety, retire in lonely groups, and in plaintive silence mourn over the sad catastrophe. But does the scene end here? No, no! When the time came which had been fixed in the counsels of eternal wisdom, to put an end to the triumphs of earth and hell—the God-head that had dwelt in him—the divinity which had commanded the raging elements into calm submission, *stood forth* in the "greatness of his strength," and said to these storms of hellish wrath, "Thus far shalt thou come, but no further: and here shall thy proud waves be stayed." "In a moment, in the twinkling of an eye," the bands of death are sundered,—the "king of terrors" is vanquished; and with immortal and God-like energy Jesus rises from the dead: thus "life and immortality are brought to light through the gospel" by the resurrection of our Lord from the dead. Thus he proclaims, as well by *deed* as by word, "I am the light of the world." And now "he ever lives" not only "to make intercession for us," but to hold up the lamp, that lights the pathway "through the dark valley, and the shadow of death," to the regions of unfading glory.

Then let our hearts' most cherished affections entwine themselves around this blessed doctrine of the resurrection. And may the Spirit of him that raised up Jesus from the dead so dwell in us that he who raised up Christ from the dead shall also quicken our *mortal bodies* by his Spirit that dwelleth in us. "Who shall change our vile body, that it may be fashioned like unto Christ's glorious body."

PART III.

THE SCRIPTURE ARGUMENT CONTINUED—THE RESURRECTION OF THE DEAD GENERALLY CONSIDERED.

Why should it be thought a thing incredible with you that God should raise the dead?—Acts xxvi, 8.

HAVING seen that the Scriptures affirm clearly and unequivocally the "literal" resurrection of our Saviour's "material body," let us next examine the Scriptural evidence in favor of the literal resurrection of mankind generally.

And here, as before, we have the testimony of both the Old and the New Testament; although life and immortality are more fully brought to light in the New. The following passage from Job is both a prophecy of the Messiah, and of his own resurrection: (Job xix, 25–27)—"For I know that my Redeemer liveth, and that he shall stand at the latter day upon the earth: and though after my skin, worms destroy this body, yet in my *flesh* shall I see God: whom I shall see for myself, and mine eyes shall behold and not another, though my reins be consumed within me." I am aware that Professor B. finds a great deal of fault with this translation, and this is characteristic of almost all who maintain false doctrines. Those who are not satisfied with the *doctrines* of the Bible, are generally dissatisfied with the *translation*, and always find a meaning by a different rendering which suits their theory: and more especially if they avail themselves of what I believe our author denominates the "*elasticity of import*;" that is, a capability of being bent during the experiment with them entirely out of their original positions—or pressed entirely out of their proper proportions, or *stretched* till they have as *little body* as the resurrection he contends for.

There are several considerations which go to show that Job in the scripture just quoted prophesies of the resurrection of the body. 1. It is connected with his knowledge that his *Redeemer*, who was then alive, should stand upon the earth in the latter days—alluding probably to Christ's coming to suffer, and to rise from the dead. 2. It is an event which will take place after worms will have consumed his body. 3. He is to see God in his *flesh*, that is, in his *material* body—his *eyes* shall see him when he comes to judge the world, and when "every *eye* shall see him." 4. This event cannot be hindered even by a total decomposition of his body, "Though my reins be *consumed* within me."

Isaiah prophesies of the resurection in xxvi, 19 "Thy dead men shall live, together with *my dead body* shall they arise. Awake and sing, ye that dwell in *dust*, for the dew is as the dew of herbs, and the earth shall *cast out* the *dead*."

In this passage Professor B. labors to show that "my dead body *means my dead body*." Correct for *once*. And how does this show that it is not a literal resurrection? Answer who can.

1. *Dead* men should live. 2. They shall rise with the dead body of the person speaking. 3. They that dwell in *dust* are to *awake* and sing. 4. Because the "earth shall cast her dead."

In Hosea xiii, 14, we have another prophecy: "I will ransom them from the power of the *grave*, I will *redeem* them from *death*. O death, I will be thy plagues! O grave, I will be thy destruction!" That this passage alludes to the resurrection is made certain by the fact that St. Paul quotes it in a discourse expressly on the resurrection, in 1 Cor. xv.

In Daniel xii, we have a prophecy still more distinct. 1. "And at that time shall Michael stand up, the great prince which standeth for the children of thy people; and there shall be a time of trouble, such as there never was since there was a nation even to that same time: and at that time thy people shall be delivered, every one that shall be found written in the book. 2. "And many of them that sleep in the dust of the earth shall awake, some to everlasting life, and some to shame and everlasting contempt." 3. "And they that be wise shall shine as the brightness of the firmament; and they that turn many to righteousness as the stars for ever and ever." Here the expression "many of them that slept in the dust," &c., is equivalent to, *as many as*, or *all that slept* in the dust of the earth. Some would be still alive when this event should happen.

We have an example of a similar use of the word "many" in Rom. v. The apostle is showing that the benefits of the atonement are co-existent with human depravity. In ver. 12, he says, "Death passed upon *all*, for *all* have sinned." But in the 15th verse he says, "For if through the offense of one, *many* be dead, much more the grace of God, and the gift by grace, which is by one man Jesus Christ, hath abounded unto 'many.'" Then again in ver. 18, "Therefore as by the offense of one judgment came upon *all* men to condemnation, even so by the righteousness of one the free gift came upon *all* men," &c. But again in the very next verse he says, " For as by one man's disobedience '*many*' were made sinners, so by the obedience of one shall '*many*' be made righteous."

Prof. B. thinks the prophecy just quoted from Daniel has the same or a similar meaning as Ezekiel's vision of " the dry bones," and consequently, that it cannot be a literal resurrection which is spoken of. That the resurrection spoken of by Ezekiel, in the vision referred to, was *figurative* all admit: for it is expressly said at the time, and in the immediate connection, " Son of man, these dry bones are the whole house of Israel." But the prophecy of Daniel will not admit of such a figurative signification for the following reason. Wherever the terms *life* and *death* occur, in the same connection in the Scriptures, they are exactly the opposite one of the other. If the death spoken of is literal death, then the life opposed to that death is literal, or natural life. If the death is a *moral death*, or a death in trespasses and in sins, the life opposed to that death is a *moral life*, or a life of faith and holiness. If the death is a *political death*, or political *adversity*, the life opposed to that death is political *prosperity*. If the death spoken of is a *death to sin*, the life opposed to that death is a life *in sin*. Every person at all acquainted with the Scriptures will readily call up in his mind numerous verifications of this principle, and he will not find an exception if he search the Scriptures from beginning to end. This use of language grows out of the very nature of the case; as everybody knows that natural life is the very reverse of natural death, and all other uses of these terms are borrowed from their literal import.

Let us now apply the principle just stated to the "vision of the dry bones." The death spoken of was both political and spiritual. The children of Israel at the time of this vision were in bondage. Their temple had been destroyed, and they themselves in consequence of their sins had been carried away captive to Babylon. Under these circumstances the vision was shown to Ezekiel. And after he had prophesied upon these bones, and bone had come to bone, and sinew, and flesh, and skin had covered the bones, and life had entered the bodies of the vast multitude, so that they stood up a great army, then the Lord said to Ezekiel, (ver. 11–14,) "Son of man, these bones are the whole house of Israel: behold they say, Our bones are dried and our hope is lost: we are cut off from our parts. Therefore prophesy, and say unto them,

Thus saith the Lord God; Behold, O my people, I will open your graves, and cause you to come up out of your graves, and bring you into the land of Israel. And ye shall know that I am the Lord; when I have opened your graves, O my people, and brought you up out of your graves, and shall put my Spirit in you, and ye shall live, and I shall place you in your own land: then shall ye know that I the Lord have spoken it, and performed it, saith the Lord."

Here is 1st, a *moral death*. The life which is set opposite to this is expressed in verse 14, "And I shall put my Spirit in you, and ye shall live." And 2d, a political death. The life opposed to this is expressed in verses 12–14, "I will open your graves, and cause you to come up out of your graves into the land of Israel, and I shall place you in your own land." 1. Their hope was lost. And 2, they were cut off from their parts, verse 11. But God would give them his Spirit; and 3, he would restore them to their own country. The language is figurative, but the reality in which the figure has its origin is a *literal* death, and a literal resurrection; so that the passage, after all, affords an argument in favor of the resurrection of the body.

But is the passage which we have quoted from Daniel figurative? If so, what does the sleep or death in the dust mean? Whatever it means, to *awake* and come out of the dust must mean the very reverse. Well then, suppose it means *political* death—political degradation and adversity. Then to come forth from this death would be to enjoy a life of *political prosperity.* But "some awake to *shame* and *everlasting contempt.*" What kind of political prosperity is this? Political shame and contempt are just what the political death signifies. Are the death and the resurrection from death the same thing? Then it cannot mean a political death. Let us see whether *spiritual* death will do any better. If the death is a death in trespasses and sins, then awaking from this death is coming forth to a life of purity and holiness. But some that were dead "awake to shame and everlasting contempt." What kind of holiness and purity is this? How hard it is to make God's word teach false doctrines!

These passages are sufficient to account for the prevalence of the belief in this doctrine among the Jews, both before and after our Saviour appeared among them. And that this doctrine did extensively prevail is abundantly evident from the history of the times, both sacred and profane. Herod's views of John the Baptist show this. A sect of the Sadducees disbelieved it, but all the rest of the Jews were firm believers in the doctrine. Paul, in his defense before Felix, declared, that "the Jews acknowledged that there should be a resurrection, both of the just and the unjust." Professor B., while commenting on this passage, says, "The Jews did *not* believe in the resurrection of the unjust." Well, Paul says they *did*, and all who think him the better authority of the two will believe his testimony. That the Jews believed this doctrine is still further evident from the conversation which passed between our Saviour and Martha in regard to Lazarus. Jesus says unto her, "Thy brother shall *rise* again. Martha saith unto him, I know he shall rise again *in the resurrection of the last day.*" Our author varies the translation here, and makes Martha say, "I know he shall rise again in the *consolation*," and contends that the Greek word *anastasis* sometimes has this signification. Now the same word occurs four times, in three consecutive verses of this conversation, with only this difference, that in two places the noun is used instead of the verb; a noun that has the same signification with the verb, and the same orthography, so far as the derivation will permit, and the noun and verb have the same relation to each other, as *permit* and *permission*, or as *baptize* and *baptism*. Why then select *one* word in the connection for *consolation*, and let the others have their proper signification? Let the criticism be consistent with itself, and then we have Martha, as soon as she heard that our Saviour had arrived, going out to meet him, and saying, "If thou hadst been here, my brother had not died. . . . Jesus saith unto her, Thy brother shall *console* (anastesetai) again. Martha saith unto him, I know that he shall *console* (anastesetai) again in the *consolation* (anastasei) at the last day. Jesus said unto her, I am the *consolation* (anastasis) and the life." To fairly state such criticism is to refute it. From these scriptures then, and many others, it is most certainly evident, that the Jews in our Saviour's time did believe in the resurrection of the body, and they used the term *anastasis*, which is rendered resurrection, to denote it. Bearing this fact in mind, let us examine our Saviour's testimony on this subject, as recorded in John v, 28, 29: "Marvel not at this; for the hour is coming, in the which all that are in the graves shall hear his voice, and shall come forth; they that have done good, unto the resurrection of life; and they that have done evil, unto the resurrection of damnation." No ingenuity can ever prevent this passage of Scripture from teaching both a future resurrection of the body, and a future retribution.

Professor Bush thinks this passage is a "reference of some" sort to the passage from Daniel which has been quoted. Well, suppose it has a reference of some sort to that prophecy. We have seen that that prophecy itself refers to the resurrection of the body. But there is no evidence that our Saviour had his eye particularly upon the passage from Daniel. He gives no intimation that what he utters was a quotation. He doubtless speaks of the same event, and his teachings, as might be expected, perfectly agree with those of Daniel. Our author has not given his views of the meaning of this passage except by implication, as we shall see more fully from the sequel. However, we can gather from what he has said, that he would have us believe that it is a *moral* resurrection here spoken of; because it refers in some way, he thinks, to the prophecy of Daniel, and Daniel's prophecy he thinks refers to Ezekiel's vision; and Ezekiel's vision teaches a *moral* resurrection. But let us see if the passage under consideration teaches a moral resurrection. As we have already seen, the *death* and resurrection here must be exactly the opposites the one of the other. If the resurrection here spoken of is a *moral* resurrection, then the death which is opposed to it is a *moral* death; that is, a death "in trespasses and in sins." To come forth from this death is to come forth to a life of purity and happiness. Well, then, "the hour is coming, in the which all that are in the graves of sin and moral death shall come forth; they that have done *good!*" What! done good? Dead and buried in sin, and yet been doing good? Is a man when dead and buried, *alive* in the very same sense in which he is dead? Dead in trespasses and sins, and yet the condition of their coming forth unto the resurrection of life (that is, holiness and purity) is their having done good, that is, having been *holy* and *pure,* while *dead* and *buried in sin.* But look at the other part of the verse. "They that have done *evil,* to the resurrection of *damnation.*" Of course all that were dead, had done *evil,* if the death was a death in trespasses and sins. To come forth from this death is to come forth to a life of holiness and purity, and yet this holiness and purity is the resurrection of *damnation!* May the good Lord deliver us from such holiness and purity. Such a construction resolves the whole passage into a mass of absurd nonsense. But let us see if the word "*consolation,*" in the place of "resurrection," will not answer a better purpose. Then the last clause will read, "They that have done *evil* shall come forth to the '*consolation*' of damnation." A poor *consolation*, I am thinking.

But it is argued that the *death* spoken of in verses 24, 25, preceding the passage under consideration, is evidently a *spiritual* death, and the *life* a *spiritual* life. 1. We deny that there is any evidence that the death mentioned in verse 25 is a moral death; and 2. Admitting that it is, we deny that it affords the least evidence, that the death spoken of in verses 28, 29, is such. The whole connection goes to show, that the death and life mentioned in verse 25 have their literal import. Our Saviour had just healed a man of an "infirmity" with which he had been afflicted for thirty-eight years. The Jews found fault with him because he had done it on the sabbath. He justifies himself by asserting his divinity, and declaring, that "as the Father raiseth up the dead, and quickeneth them," that is, brings them to life, "even so the Son quickeneth, (ζωοποιεῖ,) brings to life whom he will." Verse 21. There is no evidence that previous to this period our Saviour had raised to life any that had been dead; but he says, (verse 25,) "The hour is coming, and now is," the period was just at hand, when the dead should hear his voice, and they that heard should live. And this was literally fulfilled when he cried aloud, "Lazarus, come forth." But they *marveled* at this. Was there anything very *marvelous* in the declaration, that those who should hear his voice, that is, who should listen to, and obey his precepts, would thereby cease from their sins, and live holy lives? These were the very precepts he uttered, and which commended themselves to the understanding and the conscience of all who heard him. It appears to me, that the scope of our Saviour's argument with the Jews was this: that he being the Son of God, and being "equal with God," had power and authority not only to raise up the sick and infirm, but to raise up even the dead body, when life was extinct: that the Jews should not marvel, that he, being God, should restore life to a dead body, while its organization was yet comparatively perfect: for the time would come when all who had been dead for ages, and their bodies mingled with the elements, should be restored again to *immortal* life by his Almighty power. I say that this appears to me the obvious scope of the argument, but others may view it differently; and I will not insist upon this interpretation; but will now admit, for the sake of the argument, that the death spoken of in verse 25 is a moral death, and then show that the death and resurrection, in verses 28, 29, are not figurative, but literal.

1. If the death spoken of in verse 25 is a moral death, all the subjects of it were dead in sin, and of course none of them had been doing good; but some of those mentioned in verses 28, 29, *had been* doing good, and consequently were not dead in sins, but were dead *literally*, before the resurrection.

2. If the death in verse 25 was figurative, then those who *came out* of a death *in sin* to a life of holiness and purity, did not come forth to a resurrection of damnation: but some, mentioned in verses 28, 29, *shall come forth* to the resurrection of damnation; therefore, the death and resurrection, in verses 28, 29, are *not* a figurative or moral death and resurrection.

3. To suppose that verse 25 speaks of a moral resurrection, and that verses 28, 29 refer to the same thing, is to make our Saviour give a very strange reason why the Jews should not marvel at what he had said in verse 25. His argument would stand thus: "Do not marvel at what I have said, namely, that the morally dead, who hear the voice of the Son of God, shall live, for the morally dead who hear the

voice of the Son of God shall *live!*" Does this sound like the reasoning of Him "who spake as never man spake?"

4. But there is a difference in the *time* of the two events. The one was then present, the other was future. But it may be said, that the contrast in the two cases, and that wherein the second was more marvelous than the first, consisted in this, that in the first case only a few comparatively were raised, but in the second a great many. But why make this distinction between these passages, if both refer to the very same thing? Besides, is it any more marvelous, that a great number should be raised than that a few should, if they were all raised in the very same sense?

5. If the death in the first instance was a death in sin, the coming forth, or rising from this death, would of *itself* be a sufficient description of the condition of those who had been the subjects of this moral death; for as the *death* was a *death* in sin, the *life from the dead* would be *salvation from sin.* And in verse 25 it is simply said, "They that hear shall *live.*" But in verses 28, 29, the condition of those who rise is still further defined: "Some to the resurrection of life, and some to the resurrection of damnation."

This one passage of Scripture is an everlasting refutation, both of Universalism and of the new theory of the resurrection. I have classed these two doctrines together here, because they both criticize and torture this passage of Scripture, as they do most others relating to this subject, in precisely the same manner; and to refute the one is to refute the other, so far as this passage and many others are concerned.

But while this passage declares that all that are in the graves shall come forth, Professor Bush says multitudes of the dead are *not in* their graves at all. But who does not see that the general expression, "all that are in their graves," means all the dead? This I must say is a most puerile objection. What if some are not in their graves? Perhaps they "sleep in the dust of the earth" elsewhere. Daniel saw all such come forth. Perhaps some are in the sea. But John saw the sea give up the dead which were in it. But if there are others who are neither "in their graves," nor "in the dust of the earth," nor "in the sea," they are within the empire of death *somewhere*. But the revelator saw death itself give up the dead which were in it.

It is evident that our author had strong misgivings in regard to his theory when he compared it with the passage from John, just examined. Hear him: "This passage is undoubtedly the strongest in the New Testament, in favor of the common view of the resurrection." And why should it not be, when our Saviour set himself expressly to state the doctrine? He continues: "It is unquestionable, that our Lord speaks in this passage in stronger terms than he usually adopts in regard to the resurrection of the dead." P. 234. Again, he says, "The passage, as understood in its literal import, does certainly encounter the force of that cumulative mass of evidence, built upon rational and philosophical grounds, which we have *arrayed against any statement* of the *doctrine* that would imply the participation of the *body* in that rising again which is predicated of the dead (!) We do not, by any means, affirm that the conclusions from that source to which we have come, are sufficient of themselves to countervail the rebutting conclusions which may be formed from the present text. All we would say is, that they have *weight*, and, consequently, we are not required, or rather are not at liberty, at once to dismiss them." P. 235.

Really, this looks more like coming to himself than anything else I have found in his book. But he soon falls back upon his old train of thinking, and says, on p. 237, "So far as we are capable of forming a judgment, the evidence from *reason* preponderates in favor of an *immediate* entrance, *at death*, upon the resurrection state. This evidence we have seen to be confirmed by a multitude of passages, which yield this more readily and naturally than any other sense. But in the text under consideration, and perhaps a few others, the doctrine of a future simultaneous resurrection seems to be explicitly taught. Here, then, we are reduced to a new dilemma. [It appears he has been reduced to dilemmas before.] The character of the difficulty is changed. It is not so much now a conflict between reason and revelation, as an apparent conflict between one part of revelation and another." And now our author applies himself, with commendable zeal, to reconcile these descrepancies.

Let us now examine the process by which the passages of Scripture, alluded to in the preceding extract, are made to "yield this [the author's] sense more easily and naturally than any other."

In the first place, he has made his "rational deductions the *criterion* of *truth*, in regard to the meaning of the inspired word." Then commencing with passages which contain the word resurrection, without particularly defining and defending, in every case, a literal resurrection, he concludes that they must teach his notions of the doctrine, because they are so consonant with his "rational deductions." Now, it is not to be supposed that after the doctrine of the resurrection had been fairly explained by Christ himself, and fully exemplified in his own resurrection, which was made a pattern and a proof of the resurrection of believers, every one who alluded to it would always stop and define it, and prove that it was a real bodily resurrection. They knew that the people to whom they spoke understood it to be a literal resurrection, and no other. Such passages, therefore, are not the passages to be relied on as proofs of a particular doctrine, merely because that doctrine suits our notions, and the particular passages do not contradict the doctrine. In this way every doctrine of the Bible could be disproved, and every false doctrine that was ever thought of could be established. Suppose some other to start up, full of "progressive improvements" and "rational deductions," and assert that men have neither *soul nor body* after death. He could find a "multitude of passages" where the words "*soul,*" "*body,*" and "*death*" occur, which, in their particular connection, would not contradict his peculiar doctrine. Indeed, if he made his "rational deductions the criterion of *truth*, in regard to the meaning of the inspired word" in relation to these passages, he would be very likely to conclude that "they yielded this sense, [his new doctrine,] more easily and naturally than any other." And so of any other false notion.

We shall now see how Professor B. makes those passages, whose object is to treat of the resurrection, "yield" his own particular "sense" of the doctrine.

While commenting upon the last part of the fifteenth chapter of 1 Corinthians, and 1 Thess. iv, 17, both of which are brought in before the passage from John v, 28, 29, which gives him so much trouble, he says, "But we here encounter a great difficulty in view of our previous position, that the resurrection of every believer takes place at death, when he emerges from a material into a spiritual body. Is it not clearly implied, not to say expressly asserted, in this passage, that the resurrection of all the righteous is simultaneous, and that the event is still future, to occur at the epoch of the second advent, and in conjunction with the translation of the living saints? We can, of course, have no object in denying or disguising the fact, that these words have very much the air of directly contradicting the general tenor of our interpretation of the preceding portions of this scripture. Still, if our previous train of reasoning be sound, if our conclusions be fairly sustained by the evidence adduced, it is certain that the words, rightly understood, cannot be in conflict with them. In the present case, we are so strongly persuaded of the truth of our *previous* conclusions, founded both upon the intrinsic nature of the subject itself, and upon the just interpretation of language, that our confidence in them is in nowise shaken by the literal rendering of a passage which seems, at first view, to enforce entirely another theory." P. 191. This is the manner in which passages of Scripture, which speak expressly on the subject of a literal resurrection, are made to "yield" his peculiar "sense" of the doctrine. If the doctrine of inspiration flatly contradict his theory, the doctrine of inspiration must *yield:* that is all: for these "rational deductions" *must not* be contradicted! He concludes finally upon these passages, that the apostle Paul was mistaken in supposing that the second advent of our Saviour was just at hand, when he supposed the wonderful things which he had mentioned in these passages, relative to the resurrection, would take place; and quotes two authorities to prove it, Voltaire and Dr. Watts. Well, it is some comfort to know that the apostle was *sincere*, only *mistaken*. His *intentions* were good, no doubt. When I come to comment upon the passages alluded to, I shall produce better authority than either *Voltaire* or *Dr. Watts*, to prove that the apostle labored under no such mistaken apprehension.

We can now understand how a "multitude of passages yield" his own peculiar "sense" of this doctrine more *naturally* and *easily* than any other.

1st. He makes his "rational deductions the *criterion* of truth, in regard to the *meaning* of the inspired word."

2d. Setting out in the light of this *criterion* of *truth*, every passage of Scripture he meets must yield the "sense" required by his "criterion," namely, his "rational deductions." He meets the account of our Saviour's resurrection. The evidence of a literal resurrection, in this case, he finds is the strongest that can possibly appeal to the understanding. The account, *if true*, ruins his theory for ever. The whole affair must be resolved into an "*optical illusion*."

3d. Proceeding onward, in the light of these "rational deductions" and "optical illusions," he meets the positive declaration of the apostle

Paul, that the resurrection of the dead is a future simultaneous resurrection of their *bodies.* 1 Cor. xv, 51–53; 1 Thess. iv, 17. This doctrine, *if true,* overturns every part of his "sense" of the resurrection, which is, that it is *neither* a future *nor* a simultaneous event, *nor is* there "*any participation* of the *body* in it." What now is to be done? Here is another "dilemma." Either *his* or the *apostle's* doctrine is *false.* "Optical illusions" will not apply to this case, because it is a prophecy yet future. What then? Why, the apostle must have been mistaken! and he was led into these *erroneous views* by an opinion that the second advent of our Saviour was just at hand. Is any one so stupid as not to perceive how "easily" and "naturally" Paul's doctrine yields our author's "sense" of the resurrection? That is, *no resurrection at all?* These passages, having been *conquered,* have now fallen in the *rear,* and become recruits: and, from their having embraced the views of their new leader so "naturally and easily," they may be expected to do valiant service, in case of another engagement.

4th. Advancing again, in the light of his "rational deductions," "optical illusions," and mistaken apostles, he comes across the declaration of our Saviour, in John v, 28, 29, which sweeps to the winds his miserable theory. And now he acknowledges that his "rational deductions" *may be false;* that "they are not sufficient of themselves to encounter the opposing doctrine of this text." But now his concern is to harmonize this text with the others he has commented upon, "which teach a *contrary doctrine!*" A doctrine, however, which he has *forced* upon them by his "rational deductions," which he has made the "*criterion* of *truth,* in regard to their meaning;" but which "criterion of *truth*" he now acknowledges *may be false!!* There never was a more perfect sophism. It hardly has the merit of being an argument in a circle. If the rational deductions had been brought to prove the doctrine of Scripture, and then the Scriptures brought to prove the rational deductions which had been made the criterion of truth, in regard to the *meaning* of the Scriptures, then it might have amounted to an argument in a circle. But, as it *is,* these deductions are made the *criterion* of truth; and yet the Scriptures contradict them so positively, that it is acknowledged they may be false, and yet the doctrine is insisted on! Our author has laid his foundation in "rational deductions." Upon this he rears his superstructure. The current of inspired truth sweeps away this foundation utterly

And now, forsooth, the edifice stands firm as ever, because it has been so well put together! If it does, it is because, like the dry and faded blossoms of some noxious weeds which float in the *air*, it has not *weight* enough to *fall* when the foundation is swept away.

Our author was right when he talked of being reduced to a new dilemma, while commenting upon this passage. But the real dilemma, as we have seen, was not a conflict between this passage and others, but of a character sufficiently apparent from what has already been said.

The final comment upon the passage, which has cost the author of the new theory immense trouble, is thus given by him, in form of a paraphrase: (John v, 28, 29)—" Marvel not at what I have just said: for the time is coming when the event predicted by Daniel, whatever or whenever it shall be, shall be accomplished; and that, too, through *my* agency, to whom the Father hath given a quickening power, however lightly my claims may now be regarded!!" P. 240. What a perfectly non-committal affair is this! I submit whether a system driven to such ridiculous extremes can rightfully lay claim either to Scripture or reason.

I shall now adduce a class of Scriptures which connect the resurrection of the dead with the resurrection of Christ, in such a manner as to make it certain that a literal resurrection is meant. And here I need not repeat the proofs which have been adduced in favor of the literal resurrection of our Saviour's body. To him who *believes* the Scriptural account, these proofs are as strong as ever *were* brought, or ever *can* be brought, to establish any fact whatever: proofs that were continued for *forty* days; that were exhibited under a *variety* of circumstances, appealing to all the senses that *could be brought* to bear upon the case; and before *hundreds* of witnesses at a time. Indeed, an inspired apostle declares that they were INFALLIBLE; and not only so, but that there were many *infallible* proofs of this fact. Acts i, 3. And *proofs* the denial of which, as we have already shown, *impeaches* the *veracity* of GOD, ANGELS, AND MEN!!!

The first passage of Scripture which we shall adduce, of the class above alluded to, is in Matthew xxvii, 50–53: "Jesus, when he had cried again with a loud voice, yielded up the ghost. And behold, the veil of the temple was rent in twain from the top to the bottom; and the earth did quake, and the rocks rent; and the *graves* were opened; and many *bodies* of the saints which slept arose, and came out of the graves after his resurrection, and went into the holy city, and appeared unto many."

Here it will be observed, that although the graves were opened at the moment of the Saviour's death, yet the bodies of the saints did not arise and go into Jerusalem till *after his* resurrection. So, even in regard to these, our Saviour's resurrection was the "first fruits." The resurrection of the bodies of these saints went directly to confirm the doctrine, that our Saviour's resurrection was both a pledge and a pattern of the resurrection of believers. If the evangelist had had his eye directly upon the theory which we are opposing when he penned this account, his language could not have been more explicit: "The *graves opened:* the *bodies* which had slept *in* them *arose,* and came *out of* the *graves.* Now, *what bodies were* these which had slept in the graves, and which arose and came out of them? Certainly not such bodies as the new theory contends for; for, according to this theory, the "resurrection body is exhaled with the dying breath, and goes forth from the body *before* it is consigned to the dust." P. 178. "It *lives again, because* it *never dies.*" A strange reason, to be sure, for living *again!* Consequently, the resurrection body of the new theory *never* "slept," "because it never dies."

It never was *in* the *grave*, it *never came out* of the grave. Indeed, it never *had* any *body at all*. "It is *called* a body, because the poverty of human language, or perhaps the weakness of the human mind, forbids the adoption of any more befitting term by which to express it." P. 70.

Therefore, while this passage positively establishes the doctrine of a literal resurrection, it positively contradicts *every feature* of the opposing theory. But our author, nothing intimidated, boldly applies his doctrine of "optical illusions" to this case, as well as to that of Christ himself. "It was an appearance;" "the putting forth of a visible effect;" "they had really arisen long before." All these deceptive "appearances" and "optical illusions" having the same laudable "object in view," namely, to *deceive* mankind into the *belief* of a *palpable falsehood!* But Professor B. has discovered the cheat!!

A man needs more than an ordinary amount of grace, while dealing with a theory which resorts to such *shameful* expedients.

I have already quoted, while speaking of the resurrection of Christ, those passages which declare that he was the first "fruits of the resurrection," "the first born from the dead," "the first that should rise from the dead." But it is *not true* that Christ was the first to rise from the dead, unless the resurrection spoken of was of his body; for "simply," in the sense of "immortality or a future state of existence," as the theory contends, men had been rising for thousands of years. And it is *not true* that Christ's resurrection, being that of his *body*, was "the *first fruits* of the resurrection of mankind, unless *their* resurrection is that of the body. Here, then, as well as in a score of other places, it is seen that *both* the Bible *and* the new theory cannot be true. The theory *positively* denies what the Bible positively affirms: "But if the Spirit of him that raised up Jesus from the dead, dwell in you, he that raised up Christ again from the dead, shall also quicken (bring to life) your *mortal bodies*." Rom. viii, 11.

Now, what body is it which is *mortal?* Not the body which the new theory contends for, because that "never dies." Where in Scripture or in reason does "mortal bodies" mean anything else than *mortal bodies?* The only difficulty here is, that there appears to be a *condition* in the resurrection spoken of. On this account, this passage, and a few others of kindred character, came near making our author believe that "the resurrection was the exclusive privilege of the righteous," in which case he would have denied, as indeed he *may* hereafter, on the principles of "progressive improvement," that any but the righteous have either *souls* or *bodies* in a future state. But a little attention to this very *condition* will show that in this passage it is only the resurrection of the *righteous* which is spoken of—a resurrection effected by the Spirit of *God which dwells in them;* that is, the spirit of *love*, which will raise up their bodies like unto Christ's glorious body, making them suitable to be the companions of holy and glorified spirits, in contradistinction from the resurrection of the wicked, which will not be like "Christ's glorious body." So that if our author speaks of the resurrection in *this* sense, it is most unquestionably "the exclusive privilege of the righteous." And he would have learned this from John v, 28, 29, if he had not been blinded by his theory. For our Saviour says, "They that have done good," that is, they who have this same "Spirit of God dwelling in them," shall come forth to the resurrection of *life*, and those who have done evil to the resurrection of damnation. This *condition* then perfectly harmonizes with the whole current of Scripture on the subject. And it is probable that the apostle Paul had his eye on this very distinction when he says, "If by any means I may attain unto the resurrection of the dead;" where he employs a different Greek word (ex-anastasin) instead of anastasin. The preceding verse confirms this opinion. "That I may know him, and the power of *his* resurrection." Phil. iii, 10, 11. This is still more evident from verses 20, 21 of this same chapter: "For our conversation is in heaven; from whence also we look for the Saviour, the Lord Jesus Christ; who shall change our *vile body*, that it may be fashioned like unto *his glorious body*, according to the working whereby he is able to subdue all things unto himself." Here the apostle Paul felt what every human being ought to feel, a deep solicitude to be so conformed to Christ, that when he should come again, to judge the world, he might rise in the likeness of Christ's glorious body, in contradistinction from those who, neglecting the great interests of salvation, should "awake to shame and everlasting contempt."

Let us next examine 1 Corinthians vi, 13–15: "Now the body is not for fornication, but for the Lord, and the Lord for the body. And God hath both raised up the Lord, and will also raise up us by his own power. Know ye not that your bodies are the members of Christ? shall I then take the members of Christ, and make them the members of a harlot? God forbid."

I have given the whole connection here, that there may be no possibility of mistaking "what body is meant." Here, also, as in the other passages, the resurrection spoken of is so connected with that of our Lord, as to make it certain that it will be the same in kind with his own. Besides, this text directly overthrows another of our author's "rational deductions." He declares that "all the purposes of a future state of retribution can be answered *without* the body." But this passage declares that "the body is for the *Lord*, and the *Lord for the body*," and consequently, that "he will raise it up by his own power." Does not this look as though the Lord might have use for our bodies in a future state? And if so, "*all* the purposes of a future state and of retribution can" *not* "be answered without them."

2 Cor. iv, 13, 14: "We also believe, and therefore speak; knowing that he which raised up the Lord Jesus, shall raise up *us also* by Jesus, and present us with you."

It is unnecessary to adduce further evidence on this point. If the evidence already adduced fails to show, that the resurrection of believers is so related to the resurrection of Christ, as to make it certain that their resurrection will be the same in kind as his, we need not attempt to prove anything from the Bible.

But it is objected that Christ's resurrection can be a pattern of ours in but a very feeble sense—that there is a great dissimilarity—"a wide difference between a body with all its parts, yet entire, before decomposition has commenced, and one totally dissolved and mingled with the elements." Why not admit, then, the resurrection of our Lord, and make these points of dissimilarity the strong points in the argument, without resorting to "optical illusions?" What a strange way of reasoning is this: 1. To prove that our Saviour's body never rose at all; and 2. Show that there is a *great difference* between the circumstances of the two cases, the one being raised before decomposition had commenced, and the other, if at all, after being totally decomposed! And pray wherein consists this "wide difference," if *neither* of the bodies ever rose at all?

But we admit these points of dissimilarity, in all their strength, and shall show that they are the *strong* points in *our favor*. Because if any particular body is to be made the pledge and the pattern of the resurrection of the "identical material" body which dies, it is necessary that the body which is to be the pattern should die and rise again under circumstances which would make it perfectly evident to those for whose benefit the pledge and the pattern were given, that the very "identical material body" *had* risen again. And in order to this, it would be necessary that the person should be known, *certainly*, as distinguished from all others; that there should be certain distinguishing marks of some kind upon the body by which the identity, both before and after death, could be proved. It would be necessary that this body should rise while these marks were *fresh* in mind, and before they had been obliterated by decomposition. I put it to the common sense of all men, if these would not be the evidences, sought after by all who would thoroughly investigate such a test. Now all these evidences, in their greatest perfection, centre in the resurrection of our Lord Jesus Christ. His resurrection, therefore, is the highest proof that *could* be given for a literal resurrection of the bodies of mankind.

But I will now go a step further; and prove from our author himself, that our Saviour's resurrection furnishes this very proof. On p. 36, he says, "The simple assertion that the dead body is to be raised, does not constitute an intelligible proposition, for the reason that it leaves it utterly uncertain *what body is meant.* A resurrection is indeed predicated of *a* body; but this is a very different thing from the resurrection of *the* body, and our inquiry cannot possibly be satisfied without a more *minute* specification." Now, if the body of our Saviour had suffered decomposition, so that it could not have been identified by those who were intimately acquainted with him, it would then, according to our author's views, have been "the resurrection of *a* body." But then "this does not constitute an intelligible proposition, because it leaves it uncertain *what* body is meant." This "is a very different thing from the resurrection of *the* body." Well then, our Saviour's resurrection was the resurrection of "*the* body:" "*the* body" that was *crucified:* "*the* body" that was killed: "*the* body" which had been mangled with the nails piercing the *hands* and *feet:* "*the* body" that had been pierced with the soldier's spear: and "THE body" which bore, *after* the resurrection, all the marks of violence received while hanging upon the cross. Can our author desire "a more *minute* specification?"

He requires evidence of a *particular* kind for the support of a doctrine; and when that *identical evidence* is produced, in absolute perfection, he denies the doctrine because the very evidence he called for has been produced!! Unlike Thomas, *he* says, "I will *not* believe, *because* I have put *my fingers into the prints of the nails*, and *thrust my hand* into his *side*."

These points of dissimilarity are all our author urged against Christ's resurrection being a perfect specimen of ours, for he acknowledges that it is in some sense a specimen. But we have now shown these very points of dissimilarity are the strongest proofs that could possibly be given that our resurrection shall be like his, a literal resurrection. The new theory is most *unscriptural*, *irrational*, and *absurd*, from beginning to end. Everything in it is out of joint. Every argument proves the very reverse of what the author intended. Every missile he throws, rebounding, strikes himself, and every sharp weapon he seizes cuts his hands.

The expression, "the resurrection of the dead," so frequent in the Scriptures, must mean a literal resurrection whenever the death is a literal death. Where is the propriety of applying the expression, "the resurrection of the dead," to that which *lives* in a future state, *because* it *never dies?* In this case it should always be "the resurrection of the *living*," an expression which never occurs in the Scriptures.

Matt. x, 28: "And fear not them which kill

the body, but are not able to kill the soul: but rather fear him who is able to destroy both soul and body in hell." How can this be done if the *body* never lives again after death? The miserable Universalist quibble about the "*valley of Hinnom*" will not help the matter at all, for the body and soul are cast into hell *after* death, as the parallel passages show. And the body can no more be punished in the "valley of Hinnom" than anywhere else *after death*, unless it is raised again. And the soul does not go to the "valley of Hinnom" after death.

We now come to the celebrated discourse of the apostle Paul, in 1 Cor. xv, 3–8: "For I delivered unto you first of all that which I also received, how that Christ died for our sins according to the Scriptures; and that he was *buried*, and that he *rose* again the third day according to the Scriptures; and that he was seen of Cephas, then of the twelve: after that he was seen of above five hundred brethren at once; of whom the greater part remain unto this present, but some are fallen asleep. After that he was seen of James; then of all the apostles. Last of all, he was seen of me also, as of one born out of due time."

Here it will be seen how careful the apostle is, in entering upon his discourse, to connect the resurrection of the dead with that of Christ, and hence his first business is, to *prove* the resurrection of our Saviour. And here the language is such as to leave no possible doubt that a literal resurrection is meant. If our author please, it was the resurrection of "*the* body." "*The* body" that died for our sins. Verse 3. "*The* body" that was *buried.* Verse 4. "*The* body" that "rose again the *third* day," and not at the *moment* of *death. The* body that appeared to Cephas on the way to Emmaus, and to the apostles, the same night when he "showed them his hands and his feet." This resurrection in *this* sense he proves by the testimony of the apostles who *saw* him, *and felt* him, and *heard* him, and *ate* with him after his resurrection: and by *five hundred* others, most of whom were still living and ready to attest the fact.

Why this anxiety of the apostle to establish this truth in the very *introduction* of his argument, with a mass of evidence so overwhelming, but because he knew, that our Saviour's resurrection, so far as the identity of his body was concerned, was the proof of a *similar* resurrection of the bodies of mankind? That the apostle understood this connection, and this relation between Christ's resurrection and ours, is made certain from verses 12, 13: "Now if

Christ be preached that he rose from the dead, how say some of you that there is no resurrection of the dead? But if there be no resurrection from the dead, then is Christ not risen." Here the apostle shows that *precisely* all that can be affirmed of the body of Christ, so far as rising from the dead is concerned, can be affirmed of all the dead, and precisely what can be affirmed of all the dead, can be affirmed of Christ. He first proves that Christ *did* rise from the *dead*. And then argues that *if* Christ rose from the dead, it is absurd to deny the resurrection of the dead; *because* to deny it is to deny that Christ rose, the very thing he had proved by more than five hundred witnesses.

Verse 14: "And if Christ be not risen, then is our preaching vain, and your faith is also vain." Because the Christ whom Paul preached, and in whom they had believed, had promised to prove himself the Saviour of the world by rising from the dead. And if he had not risen, he had deceived them, and imposed upon them, and consequently Paul's preaching him, and their believing in him, were vain. Verse 15: "Yea, and we are found false witnesses of God; because we have testified that God raised up Christ: whom he raised *not* up, if so be that the dead rise not." To deny this doctrine, was to accuse the apostles and the five hundred others with *falsehood.* Verses 16–18: "For if the dead rise not, then is not Christ risen; and if Christ be not risen, your faith is vain; ye are yet in your sins. Then they also which have fallen asleep in Christ are perished." Because they had trusted in Christ to save them from their sins. But if he had not risen from the dead, he was *himself* a *sinner,* having been guilty of *deception* and *falsehood.* And those who had trusted in him to escape perdition, had trusted in one who had *himself* gone to perdition. And *every one* of these conclusions is as fairly chargeable upon our author as upon a part of the Corinthians.

Verse 20: "But now is Christ risen from the dead, and become the *first fruits of them that slept.*" No language could be more decisive and unequivocal than this. Here Christ is not only declared to be the first that rose immortal from death, but the *first* fruits of all the dead. Are the "first fruits" a pledge and a sample of the harvest? Then is the resurrection of Christ the pledge and the sample of our resurrection. And what kind of "*first* fruits" would be an "optical illusion?" Undoubtedly of a magnificent and plentiful harvest of "optical illusions!"

Verses 21–23: "For since by man came death, by man came also the resurrection of the dead. For as in Adam all die, even so in Christ shall all be made alive. But every man in his own order: Christ the first fruits; afterward they that are Christ's at his coming."

From this passage, it is manifest that the life consequent upon the resurrection is something that was lost in Adam, and restored by Christ. "As in Adam all die, even so in Christ shall all be made alive." The question now is, What kind of a death is it to which all become subject in Adam, and which is restored to all by Christ, and of which Christ himself is the "first fruits?" There are but three opinions on this subject that I know of: 1. That this resurrection is a *moral* resurrection from a *death in trespasses and in sins*, as the Universalists generally contend. 2. The opinion of Professor Bush, which is that "the resurrection is *simply a future existence* or *immortality*" of that which "never dies;" and 3. The commonly received opinion, which is that of a literal resurrection of the human body.

The first of these opinions is sufficiently refuted by the fact, that in this very connection Christ is said to be the "first fruits" of this resurrection. It follows, therefore, that if it was a resurrection from a "death in trespasses and in sins," Christ had been dead in trespasses and in sins: a notion at once absurd and blasphemous.

The second opinion is refuted by the consideration that the life which is consequent upon the resurrection was lost in Adam, and restored by Christ.

But has man no immortal part till the resurrection? Is that which "lives again in another state *because* it *never dies*," and "is immortal in *its own nature*," (p. 70,) lost in Adam? Has that died in Adam which is *essentially immortal* in its *own nature* and never *can* die? The idea is *absurd* and ridiculous in the extreme. The third opinion therefore, which is that of a *literal* resurrection from a literal death, is the doctrine of the apostle; for the body became mortal in Adam, and will be restored to immortality by Christ, who *is* the "first fruits" of the resurrection in this sense.

Thus it is seen that truth, ever consistent with itself, contradicts no other part of God's word. And we are not driven to the unenviable necessity, either of contradicting an inspired apostle, or accusing him with ignorance of his subject, nor of impeaching the veracity of the "true God and eternal life."

But the passage declares that they that are Christ's shall be made *alive at his coming*

What then becomes of the notion of a "development of the resurrection body *at death*?" But then Paul labored under the *mistaken* notion that Christ's second advent was just at hand! What a pity that the apostle should have been so misled!!

"But might not Christ's second coming mean his coming at the destruction of Jerusalem?" How will this help the matter? Did all who were Christ's rise from the dead at this time? If our author's doctrine is true, there were a good many "developments of a spiritual body at death," for there were many deaths at that time; but alas! they were the enemies of Christ who perished at the siege of Jerusalem.

Verses 24–26: "Then cometh the end, when he shall have delivered up the kingdom to Gód, even the Father; when he shall have put down all rule, and all authority, and power. For he must reign, till he hath put all enemies under his feet. The last enemy that shall be destroyed is *death*."

This passage shows that this event shall transpire at the close of human probation; when Christ's reign as Mediator shall cease. But before this, the last enemy, death, is to be destroyed. How can this be, if death holds an eternal dominion?

Verses 35–38: "But some man will say, How are the dead raised up? and with what body do they come? Thou fool! that which thou sowest is not quickened except it die: and that which thou sowest, thou sowest not that body which shall be, but bare grain, it may chance of wheat, or of some other grain: but God giveth it a body, as it pleaseth him, and to every seed his own body."

Professor Bush seems to think the objection answered by the apostle in this passage, to be made by some person anxious to learn the *manner* of the resurrection, and says he "cannot understand the apostle's reasoning, unless he means to affirm that there is something of the nature of a germ, which emanates from the defunct body, and forms, either the substance or the nucleus of the future resurrection body. . . . . Something that goes forth from the body before it is consigned to the dust." P. 178.

But it is evident from the answer of the apostle, "Thou fool," that the objector was no such sincere inquirer after truth as our author supposes. He intended to make the most direct and positive denial of the possibility of the doctrine, and to make the denial the more emphatic by giving it the form of a question; a manner of speaking very common in the Scriptures.

Thus; our Saviour says, "Ye generation of vipers, *how* can ye escape the damnation of hell?" That is, living as ye do, "ye *cannot* escape," &c. And the apostle Paul, "*How* shall we escape if we neglect so great salvation?" That is, "we *cannot* escape." Multitudes of similar expressions may be found in the Scriptures.

From the argument of the apostle it appears, that the person objecting, founded his objection upon the fact, that the body after death became *decomposed*, and mingled with other elements. Precisely the objection of our author. The objection was founded upon "rational deductions." But Paul confounds the objector by what was matter of constant experience; even a grain of wheat when sown, if it did *not* become decomposed, would remain for ever in the ground. The argument stands thus. Objector. The dead can never be raised up, the body becomes entirely decomposed, and dissolved. Its *identity is destroyed.* With what body then will it come forth? The thing is *unreasonable* and *impossible.*

Paul's answer. Thou fool! Thou objectest against the resurrection of the body, because it is dead, and *decomposed*, and mingled with the dust. But your own *experience* shall condemn you; for the very seed you sow, whether *wheat* or *other* grain, never rises out of the ground except it die and become decomposed, the very objection you alledge against the resurrection of the body. You talk of the body as being a mass of loathsome corruption. But even the grain you sow becomes the same in this respect. But you do not sow the body that *shall* be, as to this circumstance, but naked grain which putrefies in the earth, but God giveth it a body such as pleases him, differing as to the circum stance just mentioned, but composed of the same matter. It comes forth from corruption new and beautiful. So is the resurrection of the dead. The body that is sown or buried in the earth is not the same body that rises again, as to its frailty and tendency to corruption and dissolution, though composed of the same matter: *for* (ver. 42–44) "it is sown in *corruption*," in a state of decay: "it is raised in *incorruption*. It is sown in *dishonor;* it is raised in *glory*. It is sown in *weakness;* it is raised in *power*. It is sown a *natural* body," the subject of all these weaknesses; "it is raised a spiritual body," subject to none of them. For "there is a *natural* body," namely, that which was sown, "and there is a *spiritual* body," namely, that which rises again; very different as to its circumstances, but composed of the same substance.

This we conceive to be the true state of the apostle's argument, without ever being intended to give the least sanction to the "germ" doctrine. Any comparison may be *tortured* and *spoiled* by tracing analogies which were never intended. The point of comparison is a state of decay and corruption, in both the grain and the body, and the coming forth out of a state of corruption to new life and vigor. It was God who gave the grain such a body as pleased him; and the God that could do the one could do the other. "It is sown in *corruption*, it is raised in *incorruption*." What is sown in corruption? Why the *dead body*, carrying out the metaphor of the grain. "It is raised in incorruption." *What* is raised in *incorruption?* Why that which was sown in *corruption*, namely, the *body*. What else was sown in corruption? Was the resurrection body of the new theory ever sown or buried in corruption? It was never sown or buried at all, for "it escapes from the body before it is consigned to the dust." It never was corruptible at all; for "it is *immortal* in its *own nature*." It was never *dead* at all; for "it lives in another state because it never dies." It never had any *body* at all; for "it is only called a body because of the poverty of human language."

"It is sown in dishonor, it is raised in glory. What is sown in dishonor? Why, the body, in a state of dissolution, when it becomes food for worms. "It is raised in glory." What is raised in glory? Why, that which was sown, or buried, in dishonor, viz., the body. "It is sown in weakness, it is raised in power." What is raised in power? Why, that which was sown in weakness, viz., the body. "It is sown a *natural body*, it is raised a *spiritual* body." What is raised a *spiritual* body? Why, that which was sown a *natural* body. What else is sown, or buried, but the *natural body?* It is this same *natural* body which becomes changed to a *spiritual* body by the resurrection from the dead.

Will our author's nice distinction between "*a* body and *the* body" help him any here? It will only help him into greater difficulty; for the resurrection body here is "*the* body." "*The* body" which is subject to "*corruption*:" "*the* body" which is *buried;* and buried, too, in *dishonor:* "*the* body" which is sown in *weakness* "the" *natural* body. And *this corruptible, dishonored, weak, natural* body shall be raised *incorruptible, honorable, glorious, powerful,* and *spiritual.*

Verses 50–55: "Now this I say, brethren, that flesh and blood cannot inherit the kingdom of God; neither doth corruption inherit incorruption. Behold, I show you a mystery; We shall not all sleep, but we shall all be changed, in a moment, in the twinkling of an eye, at the last trump: for the trumpet shall sound, and the dead shall be raised incorruptible, and we shall be changed. For this corruptible must put on incorruption, and this mortal must put on immortality. So when this corruptible shall have put on incorruption, and this mortal shall have put on immortality, then shall be brought to pass the saying that is written, Death is swallowed up in victory. O death, where is thy sting? O grave, where is thy victory?"

Here the apostle shows that "flesh and blood cannot inherit the kingdom of God;" that is, in its frail, corruptible, perishing state; because "*corruption* cannot inherit *incorruption*," and hence the need of a change. But then the question might arise, "If flesh and blood cannot inherit the kingdom of God, what shall become of those who are still living when Christ shall come to raise the dead, and bring all men to judgment?" And here he reveals the "mystery." "We shall not all sleep," that is, we shall not all die, "but we shall all be changed in a moment." The change that will pass upon the bodies of the living will leave them precisely like the bodies of the dead after the resurrection; "for the trumpet shall sound, and the dead shall be raised incorruptible, and we shall be changed;" that is, those who should be living when this event should transpire: because "this *corruptible* must put on incorruption," whether it be a *living* body or a dead *body*, "and this *mortal* must put on immortality," whether *living* or *dead*, when this event transpires; because *frail, dying*, corruptible flesh and blood, as such, cannot inherit the kingdom of God. It must therefore be changed, and made "incorruptible" and immortal. Look at the peculiar phraseology of verses 52–54: "This *mortal*"—mortal what? *Mortal body*—"shall put on *immortality*." What else but the body is mortal? And it is the *body* which the apostle is discoursing about, as the whole connection proves. "This corruptible" —corruptible what? "*corruptible body*"—shall put on *incorruption*. What else but the body is corruptible?

Can it be affirmed of that indescribable something which rises at the moment of death, according to the new theory—that *something* which the poverty of human language will not admit of being expressed in words—that this *mortal* shall put on immortality; that this dead *something* shall be raised incorruptible? Most certainly not; for that *something* "is *immortal* in its *own nature*, and *lives* in a future state, *because it never dies;*" while the body, the only thing which is corruptible and mortal, "cannot be raised again in *any sense whatever*," but remains eternally under the dominion of death! What then becomes of the triumphant exclamation of the apostle, at the end of this passage: "Then shall be brought to pass the saying that is written, Death is swallowed up in victory. O death, where is thy sting? O grave, where is thy victory?" The king of terrors, with his foot upon the very ground that covered his victim, might lift his ghastly arm, and, showing his dreadful spear, answer, "*Here is my sting;*" while the grave, without even opening her mouth, might mutter, in deep, sepulchral tones, "And here is my *victory*."

But there is another consideration, contained in verse 52, which utterly ruins the new theory. This theory maintains that there will be no general resurrection of the dead, but that the resurrection, such as it is, is a progressive thing, and has been going on for six thousand years! But, in opposition to this, the apostle declares, "We shall all be changed, in a moment, in the twinkling of an eye, at the *last* trump: for the trumpet shall sound, and the dead shall be raised incorruptible, and we shall be changed." This shows most conclusively that the period is yet future, and at the *end of time.* Everything in this account of the resurrection is directly against every feature of the new doctrine. What language could more distinctly and unequivocally teach the future and simultaneous resurrection of the dead?

In the First Epistle to the Thessalonians, 4th chapter, commencing with the 13th verse, we have the same subject introduced again: "But I would not have you to be ignorant, brethren, concerning them that are asleep, that ye sorrow not even as others who have no hope. For if we believe that Jesus died, and rose again, even so them also which sleep in Jesus will God bring with him." Here, as before, it is seen that Paul makes the resurrection of the dead to depend upon that of our Saviour. "For this we say unto you by the word of the Lord, that we who are alive and remain unto the coming of the Lord, shall not prevent them which are asleep. For the Lord himself shall descend from heaven with a shout, with the voice of the archangel, and with the trump of God: and the dead in Christ shall rise first. Then we which are alive and remain shall be caught up together with them in the clouds, to meet the Lord in the air: and so shall we ever be with the Lord. Wherefore comfort one another with these words."

The reason Paul assigns why he would dissuade the Thessalonians from indulging in immoderate grief for their pious dead was, that Christ had pledged himself to raise them in the likeness of his glorious body, and that on account of this there would be no particular advantage in being alive at Christ's second coming, because those who should be alive and remain unto the coming of the Lord should not prevent (*φθασωμεν*)—that is, should not go before; should not be "caught up" first—for the dead in Christ should rise first, that is, before the living should be changed; and then those who were alive would be caught up *with them* to meet the Lord, changed of course from corruptible to *incorruptible*, and from mortal to *immortal*, as is shown in Corinthians.

We here have the same striking evidence as in Corinthians that these grand events will occur at a future period, and will take place at the second coming of Christ. "We who remain at the *coming* of the *Lord*," &c.: "for the *Lord himself* shall descend from heaven." The pious dead will first rise. In a moment more, in the twinkling of an eye, after the dead in Christ shall have risen, the living saints will be changed from *mortal* to *immortal*, and both *ascend together* to meet the *Lord* in the air. Nearly simultaneous with the resurrection of the pious dead, and the change of the living saints, perhaps in a moment more, will be the resurrection of the wicked, "to shame and everlasting contempt;" "to the resurrection of damnation," as is elsewhere taught in the Scriptures. It is evident that in the 15th chapter of Corinthians, as well as in the passage in Thessalonians, the apostle is discoursing *principally* upon the resurrection of the righteous. This is as might have been expected, since in both cases he was directing his discourse especially to Christians; and in the last case his special object seems to have been to administer consolation to those who were mourning the death of their Christian friends. But although Paul in Corinthians was *principally* discoursing on the resurrection of the righteous, yet he positively declares that all the dead shall rise at the same grand epoch, though not at the very same moment: "For as in Adam *all die*, even so in Christ shall *all* be *made alive*. But every man in his own *order:* Christ the first fruits; afterward they that are Christ's at his coming." The word "order," (τάγματι·,) signifies a *company*, or *band*, a *squadron*, or *co-*

hort, or *legion*. It also signifies a *command* or *order* by which these "*companies*," &c., are arranged and regulated. The apostle had no sooner declared that in Christ should *all* be made alive, than he immediately adds, "But every man in his own *order:* Christ the first fruits," who in obedience to the divine *command* or *order* rose the *third* day after death, by the power of God. This was *his* "order." Second: "*afterward* they that are *Christ's at his coming.*" These are they "who have done good;" "and they shall come forth unto the resurrection of *life.*" This is *their* order, or *command* from God: all the truly pious shall come forth in *this order* or *company*. Third: the wicked shall next rise from the dead, after the pious living are changed; but these are "they that have done *evil*," "they shall come forth to the resurrection of *damnation.*" This is *their* "order" or *command* from God; for "*all*" the dead "shall be made alive." All the wicked shall rise in *this order* or *company*, then will follow the *general judgment;* for Christ's second coming is to "judge the world." That these events will transpire in immediate connection with the last judgment is positively declared by John the revelator: Rev. xx, 11–15: "And I saw a great white throne, and him that sat on it, from whose face the earth and the heaven fled away; and there was found no place for them. And I saw the dead, small and great, stand before God: and the books were opened; and another book was opened, which is the book of life: and the dead were judged out of those things which were written in the books, according to their works. And the sea gave up the dead which were in it; and death and hell delivered up the dead which were in them; and they were judged every man according to their works. . . . And whosoever was not found written in the book of life was cast into the lake of fire." Here the resurrection of all the dead is taught in remarkably strong terms; not only the sea, but *death* and *hell*, (or hades, 'Αιδης, the place of departed souls,) gave up their dead. Death gave up their *bodies*, and hades their *souls*, that they might be united together before they should be judged according to the things done in the *body*.

In this passage the resurrection of all the dead, the appearance of the "great white throne, and him that sat upon it," the opening of the "books," the summoning of all the dead, both small and great, to stand before the throne, the *decision* which would fix the doom of all mankind for a long eternity, are but parts of one stupendous scene of grand and awful sublimity.

It is thus, by "comparing scripture with scripture," that we are able to form a correct and connected account of the grand events that will accompany "the resurrection of the dead;" and thus to fix, with absolute certainty, the period of its occurrence at the end of the world, as well as to determine the accompanying circumstances.

We have seen, in another place, that the only alternative for the opposing theory is to assert that the apostle Paul, while writing to the Corinthians and Thessalonians, labored under the mistaken opinion that Christ's second advent was just at hand, when these things would take place. But this very position, repulsive and shocking as it is, admits after all that Paul *thought* and *taught* that the resurrection would take place in connection with Christ's second advent. We shall just now avail ourselves of this admission. Paul *did believe*, then, that the resurrection of the dead would take place at the second coming of Christ: then Paul *did not* believe that "this event transpires with every one at the moment of death." But our *author believes* it. Why then has he quoted the apostle Paul to prove what he acknowledges the apostle *did not* believe?

But Paul says, in the introduction of his discourse to the Corinthians, "For I delivered unto you first of all that which I also *received*, how that Christ died for our sins according to the Scriptures; and that he was buried, and that he rose again the third day," &c. Now the question is, *how* did the apostle *receive* his gospel? He tells us himself, in Galatians i, 11, 12: "But I certify you, brethren, that the gospel which was preached of me is not after man. For I neither *received* it of *man*, neither was I taught it, but *by the revelation of Jesus Christ*." And in the passage from Thessalonians he says, "For this we say unto you *by the word of the Lord*." Was Paul mistaken in this also? Did he think the Lord had inspired him to say these things when he had received no such inspiration? If he told the truth when he declared that he was immediately inspired to say these things, then he *did not* labor under the mistake attributed to him. Therefore we see that the new system is directly at war with the *inspiration* of the Scriptures.

But that the apostle entertained no such opinion as our author attributes to him, in regard to the speedy coming of Christ to judge the world, is still further proved from his second letter to these same Thessalonians.

"Now we beseech you, brethren, by the coming of our Lord Jesus Christ, and by our gathering together unto him, that ye be not soon shaken in mind, or be troubled, neither by spirit, nor by word, nor by letter as from us, as that the day of the Lord is at hand. Let no man deceive you by any means: for that day shall *not come,* except there come a falling away first, and that man of sin be revealed, the son of perdition; who opposeth and exalteth himself above all that is called God, or that is worshiped; so that he, as God, sitteth in the temple of God, showing himself that he is God. Remember ye not, that when I was yet with you, I told you these things?" This prophecy of the apostle, relative to the "man of sin," applies in every particular to the popes of Rome. Both by *word* and *deed* they answer this description to the very letter, as could be abundantly shown if this were the place to do it.*

* "Dominus Deus noster papa. Alter Deus in terra. Rex regum, dominus dominorum. Idem est Dominium Dei et papæ. Credere Dominum Deum nostrum papam non potuisse statuerese, prout statuit, hereticum consereter. Papæ potestas est major omni potestate, creata extenditque se ad cœlestia, terrestria, et infernalia. Papa facit quicquid, libet etiam illicita et est *plus* quam Deus."—"Our Lord God the pope. Another God upon earth. King of kings and Lord of lords. The same is the dominion of God and the pope. To believe that our

But what am I doing? Has it come to this, that we are obliged to defend the inspiration of the Scriptures, sentence by sentence, against the assaults of a *Christian*, and a *Christian minister?*

There is a sense in which the writers of the New Testament speak of the dispensation in which they lived as the "*last* time," and the end of all things being at hand; but not by any means such a sense as our author supposes, as has just been shown. When life and immortality were fully brought to light by the gospel, the *last* grand dispensation was fully ushered in; a dispensation never to be changed, or superseded while man remains upon earth,—never to "wax old" and "vanish away," as preceding dispensations had done. For although the great essentials of salvation have been the same in all ages of the world, yet their mode of manifestation has been different in different dispensations. But now the system has been completely unfolded. The great atoning sacrifice has been

Lord God the pope might not decree as he decreed it, were a matter of heresy. The power of the pope is greater than all created power, and extends itself to things celestial, terrestrial, and infernal. The pope doeth whatsoever he listeth, and is *more* than God."—*Jewel's Apology and Defense, in Dowham's Treatise concerning Antichrist.*

made. "Eternal redemption" has been purchased. Jesus Christ has been "proclaimed the Son of God with power," and "the Saviour of the world," "*by* the resurrection from the *dead*." The veil which concealed from mortal view the holy of holies has been rent. "The mercy seat" has become immediately accessible through "the new and living way." We now "have a High Priest over the house of God," "who ever liveth to make intercession for us." The same divine light, which at one period was as "the dawning of the morning," and at another, "fair as the moon," has now become "clear as the sun." The same "Sun of righteousness," which in former dispensations shone only by reflection, has now risen in full view, and spreads his cheering beams over the face of creation. And he shall continue to rise, but not to set: for when he shall have attained his zenith altitude, all who have received and improved his heavenly influence shall be sweetly drawn by his attraction up to his own embrace.

Considering, therefore, this last and *permanent* dispensation of grace, with reference to dispensations which preceded it, which were only temporary in their character, and whose only object was to prepare the world for the reception of *this*—we see the propriety of denominating the present, the *last dispensation*, or "the last time."

There is also a sense in which the inspired writers speak of "the end of all things being at hand." But not at all in the sense our author supposes. When the whole of human existence is taken into the account, the longest period that can intervene between the present and the day of judgment dwindles to "an *inch* of time, a *moment's* space." A thousand, or even ten thousand years is but a *point*, compared with that flow of interminable duration which spreads itself out beyond it. And especially when it is considered, that the brief period allotted to human life is all the space we have, in which to prepare for the day of judgment, and for the scenes of eternal retribution; the period of death, so far as any preparation is concerned, brings us into immediate connection with the judgment day. In this sense, the apostles speak of the "day of the Lord," "the end of all things," as at hand, without ever supposing that it would come in the age in which they lived. And we ourselves do the same. Aside therefore from the shocking consequences involved in charging ignorance and erroneous views upon the inspired apostles, there is not the shadow of evidence that they entertained the erroneous opinions attributed to them.

We next proceed to examine a passage of Scripture which is relied upon to support the new doctrine of the resurrection, and which is the only one that with even any *plausibility* can be made "to yield" such a "sense" as the theory contends for. Matt. xxii, 23–32: "The same day came unto him the Sadducees, which say there is no resurrection; and asked him, saying, Master, Moses said, If a man die having no children, his brother shall marry his wife, and raise up seed unto his brother. Now there were with us seven brethren. And the first, when he had married a wife, deceased; and, having no issue, left his wife unto his brother. Likewise the second, and third, unto the seventh. And last of all the woman died also. Therefore, in the resurrection, whose wife shall she be of the seven, for they all had her? Jesus answered, and said unto them, Ye do err, not knowing the Scriptures, nor the power of God. For in the resurrection, they neither marry, nor are given in marriage, but are as the angels of God in heaven. But as touching the resurrection of the dead, have ye not read that which was spoken unto you by God, saying, I am the God of Abraham, and the God of Isaac, and the God of Jacob? God is not the God of the dead, but of the living." This argument put to silence the Sadducees, (ver. 34.)

The argument which the new theory would draw from this passage is the following: viz. That our Saviour proves the resurrection of the dead, by proving that Abraham, Isaac, and Jacob, were *then living*. But their *bodies* had never risen from the dead; and consequently the resurrection of the dead does not imply the participation of the body.

Now we are not disposed to admit that we encounter any "*great difficulty* here in view of our *previous* position," nor that we are reduced to any "new *dilemma*," nor that there is any "apparent conflict between this and other parts of revelation." But we shall now attempt to show that this passage is capable of an explanation, in perfect harmony with the uniform teachings of the Scriptures on the subject of the resurrection.

The objection of the Sadducees to the resur rection of the body rested on two grounds. 1. They denied that there was any future state whatever. "For the Sadducees say that there is no resurrection, neither angel, nor spirit: but the Pharisees confess both." Acts xxiii, 8. Denying that men have any *souls* after death, of course they would deny the resurrection of the body. 2. They supposed the doctrine was *irrational*, and absurd, in itself, as is manifest from the case they had supposed, and their reasoning from it. Our Saviour first clears away the difficulties which they had thrown around the subject—he answers their "philosophical objections," and then attacks their main position. And it may be well enough to notice in this case one or two remarkable coincidences, in the views of the Sadducees, and those of Professor Bush, on this subject. 1. They, like him, denied the "resurrection of the body in any sense whatever," because it encountered insuperable difficulties. 2. They could not tell inasmuch as *one* woman had had several husbands during lifetime, *which* husband she would have in the resurrection. *He* cannot tell, inasmuch as the soul has had several *bodies* during lifetime, "*which* body is meant when it is said, The dead shall rise again." Our Saviour confounds them by showing that they were both ignorant of the Scriptures and the power of God. 1. They were ignorant of the power of God; for God, who is almighty, could not only raise the dead, but could so change the gross matter of which the dead body was composed, that in a future state it would have none of those animal passions, and lusts, which had attached to it in the present life—that in this respect those who should be raised from the dead, would be like the angels, and consequently, that there would be no marrying or giving in marriage in a future state.

2. Having cleared away the rubbish which their "rational deductions" had thrown around the subject, he next proceeds to attack their main position, which was a denial of the immortality of the soul. If the very foundation of their theory could be removed, it might be presumed their theory would fall, unless, like our author's it could stand without any foundation.

Their doctrine must be overthrown by the *Scriptures.* But they had discarded all the Scriptures, except the five books of Moses. They had taken a position positively contradicted by a large portion of the Scriptures, and being too consistent to acknowledge the inspiration of certain scriptures, and yet contradict the very writers themselves, they had rejected all but the Pentateuch. In this respect we must confess the parallel fails between them and our author. Our Saviour proceeds therefore to prove the immortality of the soul from the Pentateuch itself; and quotes Exodus iii, 6: "I am the

God of Abraham, and the God of Isaac, and the God of Jacob." And his comment upon the passage is, that "God is not the God of the *dead*, but of the *living*." Thus showing that Abraham, Isaac, and Jacob, were all living when this declaration was made to Moses, although their *bodies* were all dead, and some of them had been dead for centuries. Their souls, therefore, lived after their bodies were dead. Thus the Sadducees were confounded out of their own acknowledged Scriptures, and the foundation of their objection removed. There never was an argument more logically constructed, and more strictly conforming to the established rules of argumentation, than this argument with the Sadducees.

The subject of the first resurrection, as treated of in Rev. xx, 4–6, is confessedly of great obscurity, and one upon which, perhaps, no man is prepared to pronounce with certainty. But whatever may be the meaning of that difficult passage, one thing is evident, it relates only to *martyrs* who have suffered violent deaths from persecution. For the passage commences thus: "And I saw thrones, and they that sat upon them, and judgment was given unto them: and I saw the souls of them that were *beheaded* for the witness of Jesus, and for the word of God, and which had not worshiped the beast, neither his image, neither had received his mark upon their foreheads, or in their hands: and they lived and reigned with Christ a thousand years. But the rest of the dead lived not again till the thousand years were finished. This is the first resurrection."

Whether it is meant that those, or some of those who had been put to death, when dark clouds seemed to lower over the future prospects of the Christian church, should be raised from the dead, and witness the blessed influence of a general prevalence of those great principles for which they suffered, when "the wolf shall dwell with the lamb, and the leopard lie down with the kid, and the young lion with the calf and the fatling:" when the sucking child shall play upon the hole of the asp, and the weaned child shall put his hand on the cockatrice' den: when they shall not hurt nor destroy in all God's holy mountain, because the earth shall be full of the knowledge of the Lord; or whether it has some other meaning, perhaps will never be known till the event shall be fulfilled. But whatever be the meaning of the passage, it certainly does not oppose the doctrine, that there shall be a general resurrrection of the dead, all the dead at Christ's second coming at the day of judgment, for this doctrine is very distinctly taught, as we have already seen, in the subsequent part of this same chapter.

It is therefore most certainly evident from the Scriptures, that there will be a general resurrection of the BODIES of all mankind that are dead, when Christ shall come to judge the world. Blessed be God for such evidence as the Scriptures contain in support of such a truth. This doctrine, considering its relations and its dependencies, is the most important article of our faith. All that is vital in the Christian system centres in it. To receive it in the love of it, with its relations and dependencies, is to receive *Christ.* To deny it, is to deny the *Lord* that bought us. It was on this account, that the apostles sum up the whole Christian doctrine by calling it "*Jesus and* the *resurrection.*"

An additional argument in favor of this doctrine may be drawn from the fact, that a *denial* of it involves the shocking consequences already developed in the course of these remarks.

I do not deem it necessary to enter into a separate argument to overturn the author's theory relative to the day of judgment. His denial of any general judgment is consequent upon the denial of any general resurrection. And if this last error has been fairly overthrown, the other falls with it. And if other arguments in support of a general judgment were necessary, they have been furnished over and over again by those who have so ably defended the doctrine of Scripture on this subject against the assaults of Universalism; for Professor Bush and they are at perfect agreement in their arguments and criticisms on this point.

I cannot close these remarks without entering my earnest protest against this new doctrine, from beginning to end. I regard both the *theory* and the manner of defending it as heretical and dangerous. Should the doctrine of the new theory become prevalent, I should regard it as the greatest calamity that ever befell the Christian church. It is a theory that sets up enfeebled *human reason* as *superior* to the word of God. It is a theory whose mode of interpreting the Scriptures is directly calculated to destroy all confidence in them.

It charges the apostles with ignorance in relation to the very things which they declare themselves that they were divinely inspired to teach. It boldly and flatly contradicts in terms what the apostles positively affirm.

It is a system which, while it professes to revere the Christian Scriptures, gives up the whole ground to infidelity; a system whose very motto in regard to the manner of receiving the doctrines of the Bible would be subscribed to by every infidel in the land.

I protest against the new theory as lowering the standard of Christian morals, by advocating the Jesuitical doctrine, that fraud and deception may be practiced when a laudable object is to be attained.

I protest against it, as making the hearts of God's people sad, whom he hath not made sad, by stripping from them "the hope of the resurrection from the dead;" and as "strengthening the hands of the wicked, that he should not turn from his wicked way, by promising him" that there is no day of judgment.

I utterly protest against the new theory, as ruinous to the doctrine of the atonement, by making the Saviour of the world just what his enemies declared he was—a *deceiver*.

I solemnly protest against this modern heresy, as shockingly blasphemous, in charging the eternal God, and the Lord Jesus Christ, and the holy angels, with conspiring together to deceive mankind in the most important event that ever occurred upon earth; which deception required "optical illusions" to be practiced, and positive falsehoods to be uttered: thus making the world believe, that a most stupen dous miracle had been performed, in raising our Saviour's body on the third day, when nothing of the kind had taken place; that which caused the "*appearance*" of it having been merely a *juggling trick!*

Such is the new system, and such the arguments by which it is sustained. Such are the materials of the bulwark which has been erected, from which to batter down the strong walls surrounding the doctrine of the resurrection of the dead.

But the breath of inspiration sweeps them away as the withering faded leaves of autumn are driven before the tempest. We are now prepared to answer a question asked with much assurance, on p. 247 of the book which has now been reviewed. "What then," says the author, "becomes of the Scriptural evidence of the resurrection of the body? Does it not evaporate in the crucible of *logical* and philological induction?" No, blessed be God, it comes forth, like gold tried in the fire; the brighter and purer for the fiery ordeal. But I hope our author does not think that *logic* has entered, even in the *smallest quantities*, into the composition of his "crucible." A "crucible" made up of doubtful hypotheses, apostolic mistakes pious frauds and palpable falsehoods, and heat ed only by the phantastic glare of an "optical illusion."

If there is one logical argument in the book bearing upon the subject of the resurrection, I am greatly mistaken.

I trust that it has now been shown satisfactorily,

1. That the doctrine of a literal resurrection of the human body is *not* contrary to reason, although a doctrine which mere unaided reason could never have discovered.

2. That the arguments by which the Scripture doctrine is attempted to be proved unreasonable and absurd, have *themselves* been proved to possess the very characteristics which they fain would fix upon the Scripture doctrine.

3. That the doctrine of a literal resurrection of the body is as positively and unequivocally taught in the Scriptures as any proposition can be expressed in *language:* so that if we can certainly know *anything* from the Scriptures, we can certainly know this to be a Scriptural doctrine.

4. That there will be a *general resurrection* of the bodies of all the dead, at Christ's second coming to judge the world; when the bodies of the living shall be changed from mortal to immortality, and become like the resurrection body.

5. That the bodies of mankind after the resurrection, although composed of the same matter as was laid in the grave, will be very different in their circumstances and properties from what they have been during lifetime.

6. That the good and the bad will come forth under very different circumstances, in accordance with the characters they have formed during the present life.

But in regard to the nature and properties of the resurrection body we are but partially informed in the word of God. The body that shall come forth is called a *spiritual* body, because not subject to mortality, or corruption, or change, or waste, as in the present life when it was a *natural* body. Some suppose a spiritual body cannot be material, in the very nature of the case. But why not? To become *spiritual* is not to become a *spirit;* but to become like a spirit in some particulars. Our Saviour's body after his resurrection was a spiritual body; and yet he positively declares it was *not* a *spirit.* There is nothing inconsistent in the nature of the case, in a material body becoming refined, permanently immortal, having no more need than a pure spirit to repair its wastes by constant supplies of food, as in the present life; or to rest and sleep in order to restore its enfeebled energies.

It is said of the pious, that their bodies shall be like unto Christ's glorious body. Christ's glorious body was once manifested to three of his disciples on Mount Tabor, where the "fashion of his countenance was changed," and "his face did shine as the sun, and his garments were white as the light." One of these same disciples, St. John, saw him again after his ascension, and describes his appearance as exceedingly glorious: "His garments were white as snow, and the hairs of his head like pure wool. His eyes were as a flame of fire, and his feet like unto fine brass, as if they burned in a furnace; and his countenance was as the sun shining in his strength." O what a contrast with the body that hung bleeding upon the cross! And O, is it possible that our poor perishable, dying bodies, shall be fashioned like unto Christ's glorious body? The mouth of the Lord hath spoken it. "What manner of love the Father hath bestowed upon us!" From "those eyes which have poured forth tears of repentance, shall all tears be wiped, and they shall be blessed with the visions of the Almighty. Those hands which have been lifted up in prayer, and stretched out to the poor, shall hold the palms of victory, and the harp of joy. Those feet which have been wearied in going about to do good, shall walk the streets of the New Jerusalem." Because "we look for the Saviour, the Lord Jesus Christ from heaven, who shall change our vile bodies, that they may be fashioned like unto his glorious body, according to the working whereby he is able to subdue all things unto himself." But it does not yet fully appear what we shall be, "but we know that when he shall appear, we shall be *like* him, for we shall see him as he is." It is enough for us to know that God will change our frail bodies into the likeness of Christ's body, and make them such bodies as shall please him.

Respecting the bodies of the wicked, we have still less information. We know that they shall be raised, but *how* their bodies shall differ from those of the righteous we are not informed. They awake to shame and everlasting contempt. But what effect their condition will have upon their bodies, or their bodies upon their condition, perhaps no one can tell. Some suppose that the wicked will rise, subject to all the diseases, pains, &c., which have afflicted their bodies during the present state. But I think this view is not authorized in the Scriptures. Their bodies will be spiritual. Whether the difference between the bodies of the righteous and the wicked shall result entirely from the different conditions of their souls, or from something else, I do not know that we are particularly informed.

If the resurrection body should be so constituted as to be a perfect index of the soul, this circumstance itself, without supposing any other difference in the nature of the bodies, would cause them to differ as much as light from darkness, or heaven from hell. That there is a tendency to this in a greater or less degree, even in the present life, all will allow. Long and established habits of genuine piety—of godly sincerity—of holy love—never fail, in a greater or less degree, to give the countenance a benign, serene, peaceful, and heavenly aspect. On the other hand, long established habits of gross wickedness produce their corresponding appearance. If this tendency should be carried to perfection in a future state, the contrast between the bodies of the good and bad would be of the most marked character. What could be more lovely than a body made the temple of the Holy Ghost, and filled with all the fullness of God, faithfully reflecting God's moral image in every motion, in every look, in every lineament of the countenance, in every expression of the eye,—all that is lovely in human character,—all that is blessed in religion,—all that assimilates to the divine likeness,—all that endears Christians to each other, beaming in the eye,—radiating from the countenance, and visible in every part of the body! And on the other hand, what would be more truly a resurrection to shame and *everlasting contempt*, than to be raised with a body that would faithfully expose every foul passion, every abominable propensity of the human heart unsanctified! when pride, hatred, jealousy, revenge, malignity, covetousness, hatred of God, ill will to men, with every other vice that can disgrace and blacken the human character, wrangling like so many infernal demons in the bosom, should stand out in hideous and frightful deformity, without the least possibility of concealment, upon every part of the body. But conjecture does not prove anything. Nor is it so important to us to know the precise *manner* of our future connection of soul and body, or the precise *difference* between the resurrection bodies of the good and the bad, as to be prepared to enjoy the *one* and escape the other. It is more important to know how to get *sin out* of *our* hearts, than to know how sin got into this world. It is more important to know how to escape the second death, than to know precisely the manner of future punishment. It is more important to know how to be prepared for heaven, than to know precisely in what all its enjoyments consist.

Let even the uncertainty that hangs over the *manner* of our future connection of soul and body stimulate us to seek such a conformity to the will of God—such an intimate union to *him* who is head over all things to the church, that when the resurrection morn shall dawn, when the trump of God shall sound, to bid the slumbering dead awake and come to judgment, we may be prepared to rise in the company of those "who are Christ's at his coming," and with joy ascend to meet the Lord in the air, and so be ever with the Lord. Amen.

THE END.

www.ingramcontent.com/pod-product-compliance
Lightning Source LLC
LaVergne TN
LVHW021404110826
845150LV00007B/1784

* 9 7 8 1 4 2 5 5 1 2 3 7 8 *